The United States Approach to FMCT Negotiations

Lessons for India

The United States Approach to FMCT Negotiations

Lessons for India

Dr. Md. Farijuddin Khan

Raj Publications
New Delhi - 110002

The United States Approach to FMCT Negotiations: Lessons of India

First Published in 2022

₹ 595

ISBN 978-93-92066-03-0

Published by : **Raj Publications**
108, 4855/24, Ansari Road,
Daryaganj, New Delhi-110002
Tel. : 9811010939
E-Mail: rajpublications@yahoo.co.in

Laser Typesetting : Aarati Computers, Delhi-110 009

Printed at : Balaji Offset, Delhi

Contents

Preface

From the dawn of the nuclear age, there have been several instances where successive US administrations sought to contain and restrain the spread of nuclear weapons and negotiated a host of bilateral nuclear arms control agreements with the arch-rival, the former Soviet Union. The United States was the first country to develop nuclear weapons and even used them on Japan during the Second World War. It also helped negotiate and finally succeeded in the conclusion of near-universal agreements, such as the Nuclear Non-Proliferation Treaty (NPT) and the Comprehensive Test Ban Treaty (CTBT). Significantly, while championing the cause of NPT for decades, the United States has not yet ratified the CTBT that it has already signed.

The United States, however, has not been in the forefront of countries seeking to establish a nuclear-free world until 2009, when President Barack Obama changed track. It was a tactical move. Although there had been a proposal from the Obama administration for a world free from nuclear weapons, reflected in his famous April 2009 Prague speech, it was crystal clear that the United States would not a bandon nuclear arsenals until all others did. The role of nuclear weapons in US national security policy remained intact. As the Obama administration did not abandon the role of nuclear weapons in its national security strategy, the contradiction in the US stand was visible.

The efforts toward concluding a Fissile Material Cut-off Treaty (FMCT), despite the moribund state of the CTBT, is a promising development that, if ratified by an adequate number of countries, would strengthen nuclear disarmament initiatives and hence become a stepping stone towards a world free of nuclear weapons. The United States supports an FMCT with verification provisions. It also encourages member-states in the Conference on Disarmament (CD), the principal negotiating body of the United Nations, to resolve contentious issues and make way for smooth progress in FMCT negotiations. However, the United States has certain reservations from various quarters on the modalities of scope and verification of an FMCT.

The US approach to nuclear disarmament has not been straight forward, and FMCT negotiations have been facing impasse for several years in the CD. It is a paradox that the US, one of the leading countries in the global nuclear disarmament movement, has reservations about the FMCT verification mechanism and seems unprepared to make the treaty applicable to its naval propulsion reactors that use fissile materials. There has been no official clarification on this specific issue, even though President Obama had declared that the US would seek a verifiable FMCT.

Member-states have not been able to resolve outstanding contentious issues. These issues among CD member-states need to be resolved. The US seems to understand this, but it remains adamant to any attempt that compromises US "national security interests."

The present book is based on the US role in FMCT negotiations and seeks to understand its approach toward making the treaty a reality. Various primary sources in the forms of government documents and secondary source materials, such as books, journal articles, newspaper reports, and opinion pieces, have been used as data for this book. Relevant documents from the Conference on Disarmament and other UN sources have also been utilized to make the research more authentic.

The book aims to understand the US objective, national security interests, and seriousness of its commitment to bring out a fissile material cut-off treaty that is effective, multilateral, and non-discriminatory.

It has also examined and analyzed President Obama's efforts on FMCT to understand the US motivation in realizing this treaty. It is important to note that President Obama's successor, Donald J. Trump, did make no significant move forward to conclude an FMCT. Typically, Republican administrations focus more on strengthening the US nuclear arsenals and other components of the country's military power than on arms control and disarmament initiatives. An attempt has been made to explain this phenomenon, as well.

Neither the Republican Party nor the Democratic Party permanently occupies the White House. Certain global issues continue to remain on the table of the US presidents despite the change of guards in the Oval Office. Hence it is crucial to study the dynamics of issues such as FMCT. The present book focused on the US approach to an effective FMCT when a breakthrough in the US commitment towards a negotiable FMCT was discernible.

- Md. Farijuddin Khan

List of Tables

Glossary

CD	:	Conference on Disarmament
CTBT	:	Comprehensive Test Ban Treaty
FMCT	:	Fissile Material Cut-Off Treaty
HEU	:	Highly enriched uranium
IAEA	:	International Atomic Energy Agency
INF	:	Intermediate Nuclear Forces (Treaty)
LEU	:	Low-enriched uranium
NPT	:	Nuclear Non-Proliferation Treaty
P-5	:	The five permanent members of the United Nations Security Council
START	:	Strategic Arms Reduction Treaty
US	:	The United States of America

1

Introduction

Background

The seeds for the nuclear weapons race were sown on the day when the United States decided to make an unusual yet very powerful weapon, the atom bomb, during the height of the Second World War.[1] Source revealed that the former Soviet Union, under its leader, Joseph Stalin, was well aware through Soviet spies of the US Program (Manhattan Project) to build an atom bomb. He had also seriously engaged the Soviet scientists to develop nuclear weapon capability as soon as it would be possible. The US intelligence community was not unaware of the Soviet efforts to develop nuclear weapon capability. However, the general assessment of the US undermined Soviet capability. Moscow surprised the world, including the United States, by breaking the American nuclear monopoly in 1949 – merely four years after the demonstration of US nuclear capability. The Soviet nuclear test was a signature development in the ensuing Cold War between the United States and the former Soviet Union. It alerted the US military establishment that the threat from the rival Soviet Union turned more serious, as the conventional capability of the Soviet military was not hidden from anyone.

There was no doubt that the US nuclear arsenals were very advanced compared to Soviet nuclear capability. After all, Moscow would take several years from the day of their first nuclear test to make nuclear weapons. Furthermore, Soviet nuclear experts would have to work harder to make the Soviet bombs sophisticated. However, in about a decade, the former Soviet Union, according to many experts, was able to achieve nuclear parity with the United States. Since the parity in nuclear weapons capability was achieved, the question of nuclear threat and the danger posed by the accumulation of nuclear weapons began to assume greater significance. Subsequently, by 1964, (five countries, the US, Russia, the United Kingdom, France, and China) had become members of the nuclear weapon club. The spread of nuclear capability and its impact on the security and stability of nations raised questions about the effectiveness of nuclear deterrence. The reason was that the "threat of thousands of nuclear warheads capable of destroying the human civilization over and over again hung over the world" (Blix 2008).

Jonas (2006) wrote that Washington regarded nuclear proliferation and the associated potential for nuclear terrorism as "the greatest threat to the United States in the twenty-first century." If we compare the power of destruction of nuclear warheads with other weapons of mass destruction (WMDs), such as chemical and biological weapons, nuclear weapons are far more devastating. The reason was that only nuclear weapons could destroy "buildings and physical infrastructure, and do so on a large scale" to cause human civilization to disappear from the surface of the earth (Jonas 2006). Although terrorists cannot destroy human civilization, terrorists possessing a nuclear bomb is dangerous, and the US, thus, does have concern for any threat(s) emanating from a few terrorists armed with nuclear warheads.

The US Department of State (2013) stated that the US

> "mustre commit ourselves to strengthening the three pillars of then on proliferation regime. And with respect to those three pillars – nuclear disarmament, access to civilian nuclear energy, and nonproliferation – this Administration, the United States has led through deeds, not simply through words."

Successive US governments have sought to bring in many legally binding nonproliferation regimes to formalize and sensitize the danger of nuclear proliferation. The three main legislative pillars of US nuclear nonproliferation are the Atomic Energy Act (1954) as amended, the Nuclear Non-Proliferation Act (1978), and the Arms Export Control Act (1968). While the first two legislations are to control US exports of sensitive nuclear materials to foreign countries,the third legislation focuses on military arms exports to other countries. The Act prohibits military sales or assistance to any country that indulge in nuclear proliferation activities as defined by the US or international laws. Besides, other domestic legislations reinforce the three Acts. The Export Administration Act (EEA), 1979 (P.L. 96-72) authorizes the President to regulate the private sector exports of certain materials and technology to other countries. The Export-Import Bank Act of 1945 (P.L.79-173), meant to facilitate the exchange of commodities and services between the US and other countries, authorizes the Bank to deny credit to any person or country if it does not help in advancing the US nonproliferation policy.

The Nuclear Non-Proliferation Treaty (NPT) which has more than 190 member-states, is successful non-proliferation legislation. It is at the heart of all nuclear non-proliferation regimes. However, the Comprehensive Test Ban

Treaty (CTBT) meant to halt all kinds of nuclear tests in the world has not yet been ratified by the US. Both the NPT and CTBT have their limitations and failed to rope in the de-facto nuclear weapon states such as India, Pakistan, and Israel. North Korea withdrew from the NPT and detonated its first nuclear device in October 2006. It further conducted two more tests in May 2009 and February 2013, respectively. The two most important failures of the NPT, however, are the "failure of the five nuclear-weapon statesto live up to their obligations to disarm" and violations of the Treaty by several member-states from time to time (Njolstad 2011: 7). This failure does not mean that efforts to prevent proliferation have stopped. One of the critical efforts that have been on the table for years is the goal to conclude, a Fissile Material Cut-off Treaty to ensure limiting vertical proliferation and preventing horizontalproliferation.

Fissile material, such as highly enriched uranium (HEU) or plutonium (Pu), is the vital ingredient of a nuclear weapon and the most difficult to obtain and manufacture. A Fissile Material Cut-off Treaty (FMCT), viewed by many (scholars and officials) as the next multilateral measure to halt nuclear proliferation, aim to limit theamount of fissile material available for making nuclear weapons by banning any further production of it by member-states. The FMCT was considered an additional powerful means of halting nuclear proliferation (Jonas 2006).

The Comprehensive Test Ban Treaty (CTBT) was opened for signatures in 1996 to ban all nuclear explosions. Currently, more than forty (Annex 2) countries have signed the treaty, and it will enter into force when all the signatories ratify the treaty. Eight countries have not ratified it yet. They are the United States, China, India, Pakistan, Israel, North Korea, Iran, and Egypt. The parties agreed not to pursue nuclear testing and also refrain from encouraging, causing, or participating in any nuclear weapon Explosion test. The CTBT reinforced the nonproliferation regime by banning all forms of nuclear explosion - military or civilian purposes. Previous nonproliferation treaties have restricted nuclear testing in space, atmosphere, underwater, and underground explosions.

By banning any further production of fissile materials by signatories, the proposed Treaty aims to stop nuclear proliferation worldwide.As Jonas (2006) put it, the goal aimed to keep adding restrictions until all possibilities of nuclear proliferation have been exhausted. Like the CTBT, the proposed FMCT intends to halt the further proliferation of nuclear weapons. The mandate of the proposed FMCT, however, does not explicitly mention the status of existing fissile materials possessed by the nuclear-weapon states (both the N-5 and de-facto nuclear weapon countries) though few delegates in the Conference on Disarmament (CD) have pointed out the essence for an FMCT covering both existing and future fissile material stockpiles.

The nuclear weapons states (NWS) and de-facto nuclear states have already stockpiles of fissile materials, and existing stockpiles could be converted to nuclear weapons as and when required. Hence the primary focus of FMCT negotiations has been halting the production of fissile materials by states, thereby preventing the proliferation of nuclear weapons. This is one of the main contentious issues being debated concerning concluding of FMCT in the CD.

No matter how idealistic the goal may appear, the proposed FMCT negotiations could produce confidence-building measures and declarations from all states with nuclear weapons and fissile material. This development provides a significant boost to international efforts toward nuclear nonproliferation and nuclear disarmament. International Panel on Fissile Materials (IPFM) (2020), an independent organization for arms control and nonproliferation experts stated that almost all nuclear-weapon states had stopped producing fissile materials. According to it, China stopped "production of HEU in 1987 and that of plutonium by about 1990." The proposed FMCT seeksparity and status quo from all the states to legally stop producing fissile materials. The nuclear-weapon states (NWS) except China saw FMCT as a mechanism to cap and eventually roll back the weapons programs of Israel, India, and Pakistan (Berkhout, *et al.* 1995:169-170).

There is hope that adherence to an effective cut-off by these countries would bring them technically across a psychological threshold into the nonproliferation of fissile materials regime. Also, an FMCT could provide universalization of safeguard obligations and commitment to nuclear disarmament by the nuclear haves. These could provide an easier way for the "international community to impose stringent safeguards on states such as Iran and Iraq, which are widely believed to be unreliable members of the nonproliferation regime" (Berkhout*et al.*1995).

This analysis was reflected by Burgess (2010) when he argued that besides being perceived as a step towards nuclear disarmament, arms control advocates also saw an FMCT as an essential measure that could "for the first time" bring the undeclared nuclear weapon states into the international non-proliferation regime. An FMCT would also cap certain classes of fissile material and reduce the number of enrichment and reprocessing facilities that might be targets of terrorist organizations. The United States supports FMCT negotiations and will likely to continue so with vigor and actions.What all materials and activities by nation-states are to be included, how a cut-off treaty is to be effectively implemented and how it is to be linked to nuclear disarmament are some key questions that have been part of negotiations at the CD in Geneva.

Survey of Literature

Global nuclear proliferation concerns, horizontaland vertical, cannot be addressed by any specific country or group of countries. It has, however, become a cornerstone of many countries' foreign policy. The existing literature on nuclear nonproliferation is vast and scattered. Most of them discuss various dimensions of nonproliferation issues and concerns. However, academic writings on FMCT and particularly the role played by the US in promoting it are relatively scanty. The proposed research intends to fill the gap by providing a well-connected link between general nuclear nonproliferation measures and the proposed FMCT, mainly through the lens of the United States. The literature survey is divided into three major themes: *U.S. Approach to Nuclear Non-Proliferation Initiatives; US Position on FMCT: Role of Domestic Factors; and US Responses to External Challenges to FMCT Negotiations.*

US Approach to Nuclear Non-Proliferation Initiatives

Since the beginning of the first decade of the nuclear era, the US has emerged as the leader of the global nuclear nonproliferation initiatives and tries to influence the nuclear policies of many nations in the international sphere. Global nonproliferation initiatives had started early after the Second World War. The Baruch and Acheson-Lilienthal Report of 1946 sought to establish an International Atomic Development Authority to own and control all 'dangerous' elements of the nuclear fuel cycle, including uranium mining, processing, conversion, and enrichment facilities. However, it failed due to the deep Cold War rivalry between the two superpowers (Office of the Historian 2014 a).

Burgess (2010) argued that the US did not mention in the plan when it would destroy its nuclear arsenal even if it did acknowledge that doing so was anecessity.

Citing official sources, he argued that "President

Truman did not want to accept any international agreement that might force the United States to abolish its nuclear weapons program without assurances" (Office of the Historian 2014a) that the former Soviet Union would be unable to produce its atomic bomb. To avoid the problem that derailed the Baruch Plan, President D. Eisenhower came up with the "*Atoms for Peace Program*" in 1953. The purpose was to help other countries in the peaceful uses of atomic energy.

Bunn (2003) argued that as a result of this proposal, the US Atomic Energy Act was amended to authorize nuclear assistance to other countries and created the International Atomic Energy Agency (IAEA) to provide assistance and inspectors for monitoring peaceful nuclear activities. In 1963, the USand the former Soviet Union, and Great Britain, signed the *Limited Test Ban Treaty* (LTBT) that prohibited nuclear testing in the atmosphere, outer space, and underwater. China and France refused to sign, and both the superpowers continued their quests for maintaining nuclear superiority. Although it did not produce any substantial result, it was the first agreement and an important step towards arms control. The Treaty was hailed as a success by the US as it stopped the spread of radio active nuclear material through atmospheric testing besides setting "the precedent for a new wave of arms control agreements" (Office of the Historian 2014b).

Simpson (1985) wrote that what irked the US and the international community, in general, was the 1964 nuclear detonation by Communist China. The US was hustling up its diplomatic activity to prevent any such test and further proliferation by other countries. Ultimately, it led to the signing of the multilateral Treaty - the *Nuclear Non-Proliferation Treaty* (NPT) - the basis of which was to forbid nuclear weapon states (NWS) to assist any nation in acquiring nuclear weapons. In contrast, the non-nuclear-

Weapon states (NNWS) committed themselves not to acquire any nuclear weapons capability. It created an overt international rule prohibiting NNWS from developing nuclear arsenals. The Treaty was signed in 1968 and came into force in 1970. However, the Treaty was then criticized as discriminatory by India. India and a few other countries, such as Israel and Pakistan, refused to join the Treaty.

The US was very committed to the signing of the NPT. The fundamental drive for the US, then, was to stop, particularly developing nations, who were on the periphery of the balance of powers between the two Cold War superpowers, achieving to acquire nuclear weapons. This was because the US believed the system of deterrence (Mutually Assured Destruction) that existed between the two rival camps during the Cold War would get threatened. The existing balance might also get disrupted (Office of the Historian 2014c).

Njolstad (2011) wrote that when the United States signed the NPT in 1968, it took seriously the language used in Article VI of the Treaty, "negotiations in good faith on effective measures relating to cessation of the nuclear arms race at an early date." He, however, stated that whether the United States was as committed to the other goals of Article VI – nuclear disarmament and a treaty on general and complete disarmament – was not clear as they, at that time, were not achievable in the immediate future and hence "not matters of serious political attention."

The Under Secretary for Arms Control and International Security (US Department of State (2014) stated that the US government saw the NPT as a political and legal cornerstone of the nuclear nonproliferation regime and the basis for international cooperation in stemming the spread of nuclear weapons. In Prague, on April 5, 2009, President Obama put the US perspective on NPT when he said that the basic bargain at the core of the Treaty was sound: "countries with nuclear weapons will move towards disarmament; countries without nuclear weapons will not acquire them; and, all countries can access peaceful nuclear energy."

In September 1993, President Clinton proposed for a framework which included a multilateral convention that would prohibit fissile material productions (Highly Enriched Uranium and plutonium) for nuclear weapon purposes or other explosive devices in the U.N. General Assembly (UNGA). Furthermore, the framework would put such materials under international safeguards. The UNGA adopted it subject to the critical change that the convention is "non-discriminatory," in the sense that it would apply to both the "declared and undeclared nuclear-weapon states and non-nuclear-weapon states alike" (Chow *et al.* 1995). After that, it was referred to as the Fissile Material Cut-off Treaty (FMCT).

Squassoni *et al.* (2006) wrote that the CD, as a negotiating body, responded to the UNGA Resolution 48/75L and agreed to the so-called "Shannon Mandate" (after Canada's then-Ambassador Gerald Shannon) in Geneva through consensus. The mandate called for "Ad Hoc Committee to negotiate a non-discriminatory, multilateral and internationally and effectively verifiable treaty banning the production of fissile material for nuclear weapons or other nuclear explosive devices." Ambassador Shannon specifically stated that that the mandate "did not preclude any delegation from raising issues related to the scope of the treaty – whether banning future production, covering existing stocks or adding management stocks – during discussions" (Squassoni, *et al.* 2006:4).

Sethi (1998) argued that the basic logic of an FMC Treaty was that "if no fissile material is available to countries that are already non-nuclear, they would not be able to produce bombs at any time in the future either." She further argued that there were many challenges after the end of the Cold War. The US Senate rejected the Comprehensive Test Ban Treaty (CTBT) ratification in 1999. It was considered important legislation considering its potential to halt "the quantitative improvement in nuclear nonproliferation which gave a blow to the negotiation for a new model of international safeguards proposed by IAEA."

However, Sethi (1998) pointed out that President George W. Bush's draft treaty, accompanied by a White Paper on FMCT, presented in 2006 to the Conference on Disarmament (CD), did not have any provision for an FMCT verification mechanism similar to what was espoused earlier by the *"Shannon Mandate."* This draft was overturned by President Obama in 2009 when he said in his famous Prague speech that the "US would seek a new" FMCT "that verifiably ends the production of fissile materials intended for nuclear weapons" and devices[2].

Bunn (2003) observed the inconsistencies in the US position on nuclear nonproliferation measures. For example, he said, "the Bush administration has pressed hard on Iraq, Iran, and North Korea to restrain them from acquiring nuclear weapons, but it has done so sometimes in unilateral or domineering ways that seem inconsistent with a multilateral regime like that of the NPT" (Bunn 2003: 67). To gain the agreement of the non-nuclear-weapon states, who were parties to the NPT, to the Treaty's extension in 1995, the United States also made two promises: first, not to use nuclear weapons against non-nuclear-weapon NPT parties unless they attack the United States while in alliance with another nuclear-weapon state; and second, the US agreed to pursue "progressive efforts to reduce nuclear weapons globally, with the ultimate goal of eliminating those weapons."

However, in its Nuclear Posture Review of 2001 and its National Strategy on Weapons of Mass Destruction of 2002, President Bush administration made clear that the United States was prepared to use nuclear weapons against a non-nuclear-weapon NPT party. The above promises were again shredded by President George W. Bush's decision to withdraw the Anti-Ballistic Missile (ABM) Treaty in 2002.

Holloway (2011) summed up the debate in the US, which had shaped contemporary American thinking and US policy to an extent. He pointed out three main issues in the debate. They were: issues on having a vision of the nuclear-weapons-free world, the feasibility of such a vision,and debates on the connection "between nuclear disarmament and nuclear nonproliferation." The second chapter elaborated on the three main issues in the debate.

US Position on FMCT: Role of Domestic Factors

The US sees that global nuclear proliferation would lead to a dangerous and unstable world. The US has been at the forefront since the end of the Second World War to stop, or at least slowdown, the spread of nuclear proliferation worldwide.

Chow, Brian G. *et al.*(1995) stated that one objective of the then nonproliferation policy was to cap and eventually reversethe nuclear-weapon programs in the undeclared nuclear weapons states, viz. India, North Korea, and Pakistan, none of whom had publicly revealed their status as nuclear states in 1995. Another objective was to prevent terrorists and other sub-national groups from gaining access to nuclear weapons or sensitive nuclear materials - plutonium or highly enriched uranium (HEU). Indeed, since the question of the possibility of nuclear weapons and devices falling into the hands of non-state actors and terrorist outfits that are Radically against the US and its foreign policy became evident, the US became more concerned. American presidents had acknowledged the threat posed by them.

Burgess (2010) argued that the ultimate purpose of an FMCT is to contribute to fulfilling of the goal of nuclear disarmament by restricting the production of weapons-grade fissile materials, that is, plutonium and HEU. Nevertheless, the pursuit of cut-off proposals after the Cold War was pushed to the background "as the importance of the testing and production of nuclear weapons became evident." The fear of nuclear pollution caused by nuclear tests overshadowed the FMCT proposal. Following the conclusion of CTBT negotiations in 1996, FMCT appeared to be thenext priority, yet CD members could not agree on a program of work. The reason for this lies within the CD's four areas of work - nuclear disarmament, prevention of arms race in space (PAROS), negative security assurances and a fissile material production cut-off competed for priority (Squassoni, *et al.*2006).

Kimball (2013) stated that the non-nuclear weapons states that were parties to the NPT were prohibited from producing or acquiring fissile materials for nuclear weapons. "An FMCT wouldprovide new restrictions for the five recognized nuclear-weapon states (NWS) – the US, Russia, the United Kingdom, France, and China, and for the four nations that are not NPT members (Israel, India, Pakistan, and North Korea)."

Udgaonkar (1999) wasskeptical about the proposed Treaty being a successful one without any substantial commitment from the "nuclear haves." He argued that in the UNGA resolution (1993), which set in motion the negotiations of FMCT, there was no mention of the aim of nuclear disarmament. As far as Nuclear Weapons States (NWS) are concerned, they have not shown any commitment on their part of bargain related to the NPT. The US position has been that of relying on nuclear weapons to defend its security. From the American perspective, at a minimum, to enter into an FMCT, the United States must determine that its stocks are adequate to meet any future military requirement, especially for a potentially-unlimited duration treaty.

In May 2006, President George W. Bush administration presented the first draft treaty for an FMCT which omitted verification provisions, consistent with the US position that the so-called "effective verification" of an FMCT cannot be achieved. The Administration's White Paper on FMCT stated that the US had concluded that the extensive verification mechanisms and provisions could compromise core US national security, and many countries would be hesitant to implement them. The White Paper stated that the US believed the CD should avoid focusing on "time consuming" and "futileefforts" tonegotiate "effective" verification and instead should focus only on "realistic objectives" to create the conditions necessary for negotiating an FMCT.

Reif and Foley (2009), rejecting the US approach set forth by the Bush administration in May 2006, argued that they had supported the approach advocated by the privately organized International Panel on Fissile Materials (IPFM). The IPFM's proposal, they argued, included verification of an FMCT covering both future production and pre-existing stocks. The IAEA Safeguards Division would oversee these. The IAEA Safeguard Division would have to expand its operation, and the IAEA's larger budget needed could be incurred by member countries.

International Panel for Fissile Material (2009)[3] explained why it preferred an internationally effective, verifiable treaty. It stated that a verified treaty would boost the confidence in FMCT and address the so and so perceived discrimination by the NPT between nuclear-weapon states And non-nuclear-weapon states. Moreover, it said that international verification of an FMCT would make "an important contribution to establishing an effective verification system for future nuclear disarmament measures."

Jonas (2006), however, argued that such criticism of administration's position appeared politically motivated as many countries saw the U.S.'s clear commitment to treaty negotiations. He said that the US wanted to see the proposed treaty move in the form of a treaty so that the objective of reducing nuclear stockpiles leading to disarmament and equity between NWS and NNWS were achieved.

However, President Bush administration's position on verification was reversed by his successor President Obama when he said in his April Prague speech (2009) that "the US would seek a treaty that verifiably ends the production of fissile materials intended for use in state nuclear weapons..." The United States had, thus, indicating the willingness to overcome the existing impasse by pursuing FMCT negotiations outside of the Conference on Disarmament (CD), operating instead through informal and formal discussions. This development was a heralding change in the US position and its policy approach to nuclear non-proliferation policy that seemed to have given the green signal for an intrusive verification treaty and, thus, fully committed itself to a multilateral, non-discriminatory, and effectively verifiable treaty.

Reif and Foley (2013) stated that within the United States, bipartisan support exists for a verifiable FMCT. The bipartisan Congressional Commission on the *Strategic Posture of the United States*, and the *Councilon Foreign Relations Task Force on US Nuclear Weapons Policy*, endorsed a verifiable treaty that ends the production of fissile material for weapons purposes. On June 3,2009, in a Senate floor statement, Senator McCain endorsed an FMCT by emphasizing the role of the IAEA to use the tools to ensure a world free of Nuclear weapons.

However, Reif and Foley (2013) argued that strong Republican opposition to "Obama's nuclear disarmament proposal persists, with former Senator John Kyl (R-AZ) and Senator Jeff Sessions (R-AL) having led the charge against the Comprehensive Test Ban Treaty (CTBT)." So, it is to see if enough Republicans would support a verifiable FMCT to ensure ratification.

Ma and Hippel (2001) argued that should the United States convert HEU to LEU as reactor fuel, as France did, "it could then meet the proposed requirements of the FMCT as delineated by those who advocate extending the FMCT to the production of fissile material for naval propulsion." Ma and von Hippel regarded converting from HEU to LEU as reactor fuel desirable; however, the United States Navy did not view it as such (Burgess 2010:14).

Burgess (2010) argued that the suggested conversion to LEU had certain vital disadvantages for the US Navy and the US Navy had strong reservations about the mandate of the proposed FMCT that would include nuclear propulsion in strategic submarines and the involvement of the IAEA. He argued, for example, according to a report to the US Congress in 1995, the Director of the Office of Nuclear Propulsion (ONNP) stated that replacing by LEU would reduce the core life for Trident-class submarines and Nimitz-class aircraft carriers equipped with 45-year cores, to 14 and 10.4 years respectively. In this light, Burgess wrote that the US Navy had adopted a prudent and cautious approach keeping in military reserve all the fissile material usable for naval propulsion.

US Responses to External Challenges to FMCT Negotiations

The proposed FMCT is considered the next step in the

nuclear nonproliferation regime. Many commentators have stated that the longer the FMCT stays as a mere concept, the greater the damage to the NPT. There are several external challenges to an effective FMCT, and the US responses to these have been amorphous.

An analysis of FMCT by the Nuclear Threat Initiative (NTI)[4](2018) stated that two primary issues divide thedifferent views for an effective FMCT: verification and pre-existing stocks. Concerning the issue of pre-existing stocks, under the 2009 International Panel on Fissile Materials' (IPFM) proposal, verification of an F.M.(C).T.[5] covers both future production and pre-existing stocks. "These would be overseen by the IAEA Safeguards Division and cover uranium enrichment facilities, reprocessing façilities, material declared in excess for military use, and HEU for use in naval-propulsion reactor fuel" (Reifand Foley 2013).

About compliance, the verification issue is what separates differing views on FMCT. Under the NPT, non-nuclear-weapon states (NNWS) have already committed not to produce fissile material for weapons and are under verification requirements by the IAEA. Therefore, the obligations of an FMCT would primarily impose limitations on the five declared nuclear-weapon states under the NPT (China, France, Russia, the US, and the United Kingdom) as well as the four countries currently outside the NPT (India, Israel, North Korea, and Pakistan). If all or most of these states do not participate in the treaty negotiations, a cut-off treaty will not hold much value. Many view the participation of India, Israel, Pakistan, and North Korea in the verification process as a crucial step so that the proposed fissile material cut-off treaty would legally bring them into the fold of the international nonproliferation regime.

Burgess (2010) argued that the building of a regime that would have necessary financial support, as well as the capability to verify a country's capacity to producefissile materials, is a distant project. The strict and intrusive verification measures outlined under the proposed FMCT would hurt the US national interest as the US, like Russia, has strict reservations about revealing the core policy on fuel cycle and naval reactors being scanned by external agencies. Moreover, other N-5 member states would not accept the FMCT (intrusive) verification for naval propulsion. Moreover, he argued that the pledges given by the US that no fuel ever put under the international safeguards would be withdrawn for military purposes did not apply to the US Navy.

Jonas (2006) opined that besides thenegotiating-burden,which seems to be a cause of not progressing, the concern of foreign spies in the guise of nuclear inspectors was an important aspect thatthe US did notwant to take a risk. This is because safeguardsand inspectionsare done multilaterally under the banner of an international specialized organization. Hence, the US does not want to risk something it has been proceeding with extreme caution. He further argued that given the difficulty of resolving any one of the issues, deletion of a verification regime, undoubtedly one of the most contentious matters in an FMCT, could pave the way for successful negotiations rather than impedeprogress.

Maand Hippel (2001)argued that the United States could comply with their proposed version of an FMCT by banning the production of fissile materials for weapons and extending it to any weapons-usable fissile materials for any military use, including naval propulsion reactors. They further argued that if the FMCT were to be upheld by allparties, countries joining the nuclear navy propulsion "club" would have to switch their fuel supply toLow Enriched Uranium (LEU). They, citing the French example, opined that the US could shift from HEU to LEU.

Tellis (2001) wrote that since the Cold War ended, the

nuclear rivalry subsided and there had been a movement Toward "low salience of nuclear environment", which was as per the Indian strategic interests. India, for this reason, generally argued for a "progressive drive" in the direction of complete nuclear disarmament. However, he wrote that there was hardly any conflict between the United States and India on the need to curb nuclear proliferation. Moreover, primary India's opposition to the United States' nonproliferation policy has been on its application than" toward its general logic."

Thus, even if India has not signed the NPT and the CTBT, "India remains committed in principle to supporting a Fissile Material Cut-off Treaty (FMCT)", assuming it to be a treaty that would support the nuclear nonproliferation regime. Nevertheless, it is unlikely to sign an agreement requiring India to open up to the complete verification of existing stockpiles. This is because he explained that a hegemonic power like the United States would influence the policymaking of any foreign country concerning its nuclear decision-making. This also applies to any freedom of choiceon nuclear decision-making that "India nationally enjoys" (Tellis 2001).

Nayan (2011) observed that India expected that countries "must stick to the 1993 resolution that favors a treaty banning future production of fissile material." India rejected the 2006 US FMCT draft favoring a treaty without a verification regime in Conference on Disarmament (CD) as it believed an effective verification mechanism would ensure detection, deterrence, and full compliance to the safety concerns.

Glaser (2012) opined that initial national declarations of fissile material holdings – HEU and plutonium – would be a starting point toward nuclear disarmament efforts which would be enriched by better ground-work data in the nuclear arsenals. A robust verification approach would ultimately require inspectors to have access to fissile material production and storage site. This can be done in three levels viz. - independent assessment by states, then cooperating approaches and nuclear archaeology[6] and finally toward full disclosure, which would make a purpose ful impact.

While a "ban on the production of fissile material for nuclear weapons or other nuclear explosive devices" implies a cut-off, several states often call for a Fissile Material Treaty (FMT) that would limit existing stockpiles of fissile material in addition to future production. The *Shannon Mandate* did explicitly not preclude these states from raising this issue in negotiations. In this manner, an effective FMCT would promote the principles of both nonproliferation and disarmament.

Sethi (1998) stated that the US, Canada, the U.K., and France viewed the mandate as being confined only to the "future production of fissile material for weapons besides insisting on a delinking of the issue with that of disarmament." The U.K. and France also insisted that the treaty must not limit their production of plutonium and HEU put to civilian use. While India supports this position, it differs on the issue of linkage of the FMCT with nuclear disarmament. India and Pakistan have been insisting on linking "fissban" to the broader objective of disarmament and hence a link to CD's negotiations of an FMCT.

Berkhoutand Bukharin (1995) addressed the primary concern of some countries that the proposed FMCT might serve as a legitimizing platform for de-facto nuclear weapons states like India, Pakistan, and a few others. They argued that legitimizing the status of the de-facto NWS would not be a helpful precedent as it might allow the de-facto nuclear-capable states to avoid pressures to join NPT. To avoid this, they opined that the practical draft should not leave any scope for the de-facto nuclear weapon states to escape joining the NPT while becoming a member of FMCT easily as "unsafeguarded stockpile states."

The background research was based on two primary hypotheses:

- The proposed FMCT serves as a stepping stone towards the goal of general and complete disarmament, particularly, nuclear disarmament.
- The proposed FMCT aims at an effective and non-discriminatory regime.

The main objectives of the research have been:

- To understand the ultimate goal of the proposed FMC Treatyandthenatureofobstaclestoaneffective FMCT.
- To examine the US position and commitment to the ongoing negotiation for an FMCT and the elimination of nuclear weapons in general.
- To critically analyze the nature and types of obstacles or challenges before the USobjectively.
- To understand and bring out the overall impact of an effective FMCT on the general goal of a nuclear-free world.

The book has attempted to answer the following research questions:

- What is the ultimate goal of FMCT, and how is itdifferent from other non-proliferation treaties?
- What is the US position on the proposed FMC Treaty? Why the US needs to have an effective and verifiable cut-offtreaty?
- Is the US serious in committing itself to bringout a cut-off treaty that is non-discriminatory and sets a standard whereby all countries commit to stemming nuclear weapons proliferation as targeted?

- How would the US resolve the two conflicting interests between a commitment for an effective multilateral cut-off treaty on the one hand and concerns about compromising its national security in the process; on the other hand?
- Will the proposed Treaty be another US-imposed treaty designed for some countries to fall in line without any genuine commitment towards nuclear disarmament?

Notes

1. After Physicist Albert Einstein's signed letter to the then President Franklin D. Roosevelt(1939) warning the President of a threat coming from Nazi Hitler's possible Atomic Bomb Project, the President initiated, further propelled by the Pearl Harbor attacks in 1941, the Manhattan Project which ended with the US testing (code-named "Trinity") the first atomic bomb in the history.
2. Later, inherre marks at the Review Conference of the Nuclear Nonproliferation Treaty in the United Nations in May 2010, the then Secretary of State, Mrs. Hillary Clinton, stated that the United States was "past ready to start multilateral negotiations on a verifiable Fissile Material Cut off Treaty."
3. The International Panel on Fissile Materials (IPFM) was founded in January 2006 and is an independent group of arms-control and nonproliferation experts from both nuclear weapon and non-nuclear-weapon states.

   The Panel has been co-chaired since 2015 by Professor Alexander Glaser and Dr. Zia Mian of Princeton University and Professor T. Suzuki of Nagasaki University, Japan. Previously, it was co-chaired by Professor Jose Goldemberg of the University of Sao Paolo, Brazil (2006-2007), Dr. R. Rajaraman (2007-2014), Professor Emeritus of Jawaharlal Nehru University, New Delhi, India, and Professor Frank von Hippel of Princeton University (2006-2014). Princeton

University's Program on Science and Global Security provides administrative and research support for the IPFM.

4. The Nuclear Threat Initiative (NTI) is a nonprofit, non-partisan organization with a mission to strengthen global security by reducing the risk of use and preventing the spread of nuclear, biological, and chemical weapons and to work to build the trust, transparency, and security that are preconditions to the ultimate fulfillment of the Non proliferation Treaty's goals and ambitions. It was founded in 2001 by philanthropists Ted Turner (Co-Chair) and former US Senator Sam Nunn (Co-Chair and CEO of NTI). Some of the other leading Board members of NTI are former Secretary of Defense William J. Perry; former US Senator Richard J. Lugar; Nobel Laureate Amartya Sen, and others (*Source:www.nti.org*).

5. There is an apparent disagreement as to the usage of the term– "FMCT." States in the CD that favor including fissile stockpiles tend to call for a Fissile Material Treaty (FMT), where as those favoring a complete ban on production seemto like to call it Fissile Material Cut-Off Treaty (FMCT). The IPFM designation" F.M.(C)T" seems to indicate the disagreement in the usage correctly.

6. According to Glaser(2012), nuclear archaeology is a process that involves "measurements made at waste storage and former production sites and be tailored to the particular type of material (plutoniumor HEU) and production process used. An established tool for this process is the graphite iso to pe-ratio method(GIRM),which is based on measuring the levels of transmutation products found in the graphite of graphite-moderated plutonium production reactors.

2

US Approach to Nuclear Non-Proliferation Initiatives

Since the beginning of the first decade of the nuclear era, the US has emerged as the leader of the global nuclear non-proliferation initiatives and tries to influence the nuclear policies of many nations in the international sphere. The US leads its support in the global disarmament initiatives. It also intends to improve the existing regimes by adding up a few more layers to them, including effective multilateral treaties to fill any gap in its efforts towardscontaining nuclearproliferation.

Before proceeding to examine and analyze the US approach to nuclear non-proliferation initiatives, one pertinent question needs to be addressed as to why the US is keen to prevent nuclear proliferation. What makes the US committed to build up domestic laws, sign treaties with nations, and support most ardently the global nuclear non-proliferation regime? Nuclear weapons have been a central point of discussion in the US foreign and national security making process since the start of the Cold War.

Three different reasons can be assessed. First, military

use of nuclear energy has been the foremost concern dominating the US government thinking and policy-making since the early era of nuclear weapons. The US has never yielded control of nuclear warheads to other states. This comes from the logic that nuclear weapons are unique and "something to be contained, guarded and restricted." The Atomic Energy Act (1946), later amended in 1954, enjoins the belief that nuclear power contains the seeds of great harm. So it is in the United States' interest and global welfare to stop its spreading (Brenner 1981:2).

The second reason is that "weapons of mass destruction (WMD), including, nuclear, chemical and biological weapons and missiles, especially in the hands of radical states and terrorists, are considered by the US as a major threat to US national security interests" (Nikitin*et al.* 2012). The Department of State (2013) stated that "The proliferation of Weapons of Mass Destruction (WMD) and related materials, technologies, and expertise - and the fact that terrorists are trying to acquire them - is a preeminent challenge to American national security... ". Nikitin *et al.*(2012) stated that the United States "has led the international community in establishing regimes to check the proliferation of nuclear, chemical, and biological weapons and missiles."

Finally, nuclear weapons still play an essential role in the US national security policy even after the demise of the former Soviet Union. The George W. Bush administration argued that his "tailored deterrence"[1] approach would deter many "potential" aggressors from taking any action against the US or its allies and hence persuaded them not to tread nuclear weapons or other WMDs paths. Many critics pointed out that this was against the US pledge in the Nuclear Non- Proliferation Treaty (1968) that it would reduce the role of nuclear weapons in security policy. Further, they argued that The approach might undermine US nuclear non-proliferation efforts by projecting such nuclear posture in its defense and foreign policy (Woolf 2003: 6). To shun such criticisms which might bring trouble to the US policy, it seemed imperative for Washington to champion the case of nuclear non- proliferation at the worldstage.

The proposed FMCT, which is under negotiations is an outcome towards this direction. However, the US approach to nuclear non-proliferation has been shrouded with much ambiguity. For example, during the Bush administration, the US signed a nuclear weapons planning guidance that explicitly states that the United States might use nuclear weapons against any adversary (ies) in response to chemical or biological weapons against it or its allies (Kristenson 2005: 108). This is to say that the US has never adopted a "no first-use policy" in its nuclear policy (Woolf 2008:13). The mismatch between its intention and corresponding action is often exposed signaling a mixed message to potential proliferators in the international system.

Nevertheless, the US policies on nuclear non-proliferation serve as a pivot as the US leadership on a global platform has been a catalyst to prevent the spread of nuclear weapons. Much of the success in concluding such an effective and multilateral treaty harps on the US approach to negotiating table in the Conference on Disarmament (CD). The approach has not been, nevertheless, consistent. Successive Presidents have their ways to deal with non-proliferation issues and accordingly formulate their policies and strategies. At times strategic and economic interests become a priority, and nuclear non-proliferation policies remain at the backseat and at other times compromised.

Few fundamental questions arise at this stage, such as whether US foreign policy operates with non-proliferation efforts as the top priority. If yes, why the US Senate has not Ratified Comprehensive Test Ban Treaty (CTBT), despite President Obama's pledge in April 2009 to pursue US CTBT ratification "immediately and aggressively." If not, why it is concerned with establishing an effective and multilateral treaty like FMCT to halt production of fissile materials. President Obama's announcement that his administration was willing to agree to a verification regime to conclude the ongoing negotiations on FMCT successfully was a complete U-turn from the position held by his predecessor. That was a shot in the arm for the negotiating members in the CD. Then also it was not clear whether President Obama would win over the intense opposition from US armed forces, particularly the US Navy, and navigate further towards its successful conclusion.

The chapter is divided into two interrelated and important parts. The first part has highlightedthe methods involved in the US approach to nuclear non-proliferation initiatives. These methods often incorporate US domestic laws and legislations, international treaties and other global non-proliferation regimes. The second part deals with the success and failure of the non-proliferation initiatives adopted to halt nuclear proliferation. It has highlighted several decisions by various administrations to delineate further the arguments made. These parts are systematically and coherently explained and concluded in a manner to enable a link between the US approach to nuclear non-proliferation initiatives and prospects of the FMCT negotiations.

Before proceeding towards the US domestic laws governing non-proliferation issues, it is important to highlight some of the significant early initiatives taken by the US to channelize the use of nuclear powers. Concerned about the security and stability of the nuclear weapons after the end of the Second World War, the US government volunteered to help in the study of nuclear energy efforts that became the foundation for the Baruch Proposal. Three studies are the Jeffries Report, the Franck Report, and the Acheson- Lilienthal Report (Burgess 2010: 8).

Baruch Plan: On June 14, 1946, before a session of the United Nations Atomic Energy Commission (UNAEC), US representative Bernard Baruch[2] presented a proposal for the creation of an international Atomic Development Authority (Office of the Historian 2013). According to the US Department of State (2013),

> "Under the Baruch Plan, the Atomic Development Authority would oversee the development and use of atomic energy, manage any nuclear installation with the ability to produce nuclear weapons, and inspect any nuclear facility conducting research for peaceful purposes. The plan also prohibited the illegal possession of anatomic bomb; the seizure of facilities administered by the Atomic Development Authority, and punished violators who interfered with inspections. The Atomic Development Authority would answer only to the Security Council, which was charged with punishing those nations that violated the terms of the planby imposing sanctions. Most importantly, the Baruch Plan would have stripped all members of the United Nations Security Council of their veto power concerning the issue of United Nations sanctions against nations that engaged in prohibited activities. Once the plan was fully implemented, the United States was to begin the process of destroying its nuclear arsenal"(Office of the Historian 2013).

Given the nature of the relationship between the United States and the former Soviet Union after the Second World War, President Truman was not willing to concede any attempt by the Soviets to have an international agreement requiring the United States to abolish its nuclear weapons program without any valid assurance that the Soviets would be unable to produce an atomic bomb. The former Soviet Union, on the other hand, opposed any plan that would retain the US Nuclear monopoly and also was against international inspections of the Soviet domestic nuclear facilities. Moreover, the Soviets thought it would interfere with the national sovereignty and internal affairs of states and that the provision denying a permanent member of the Security Council the right of veto was contrary to the UN Charter (Roberts 2001: 22). As anticipated by the United States, the Polish and former Soviet Union's abstentions on December 30, 1946, UNAEC vote thwarted the adoption of the Baruch Plan.

Atoms for Peace: The United States was shocked at the former Soviet Union's first explosion of a nuclear device in 1949, much before the US had anticipated. The big question that was on the minds of the leaders of the United States was whether the Soviets would use their nuclear forces against the United States, and if so, when (Burgess 2010: 16). To avoid the problem that derailed the Baruch Plan, President D. Eisenhower presented his *"Atoms for Peace"* plan at the United Nations in 1953. The goal of the plan was to advance the peaceful uses of atomic energyalong with nuclear disarmament by transferring fissile material from military to civiluses.

In his address to the UN General Assembly on December 8, 1953, the President stated

> "... The governments principally involved, to the extent permitted by elementary prudence, should begin now and continue to make joint contributions from their stockpiles of normal uranium and fissionable materials to an international atomic energy agency. The more important responsibility of this atomic energy agency would be to devise methods whereby this fissionable material would be allocated to serve the peaceful pursuits of mankind..."(UNGA Presidential Address 1953).

Bunn (2006) stated that, by implication, it could only mean seeking an agreement to halt the production of fissile materials for military purposes. Its purpose was also to

Provide "assistance to other countries in the peaceful uses of atomic energy." Subsequently, the US Atomic Energy Act (1946) was amended in 1954. The International Atomic Energy Agency (IAEA) was established in 1956 to provide "both assistance and inspectors for peaceful nuclear activities." Great care was taken to enable the IAEA to perform surveillance activities over nuclear facilities of member states with authority (Brenner 1981:5).

Brenner (1981) argued that the Baruch Plan, President Eisenhower's Atoms for Peace, creation of the IAEA, and negotiations of the Nuclear Non-Proliferation Treaty (NPT) were all meant to contribute towards the development of a global system for managing peaceful nuclear energy. It was done with a conscious effort to give political meaning anddirection "on the technical and institutional arrangements for developing and transferring civilian technology" (Brenner 1981). He further argued that this was the US government's attempt to keep the two sides of nuclear energy- civilian and military applications of nuclear power-in "watertight compartments." Thus, the arrangements between the United States and others receiving technical nuclear aid or purchasing nuclear products were the outcome of the belief that nuclear energy can be harnessed at the maximum level for civilian use while keeping the principle of weapons abstention intact.

In the 1950s and 1960s[3], there were several proposals for the prevention of the proliferation of fissile materials for military uses. However, the continuing deep mistrust between the two superpowers did not allow any further improvement in halting proliferation; instead, the period saw massive stockpiling of nuclear weapons and the production of fissile materials. The last official statement by the US urging a fissile material production cut-off came in 1969 at the Eighteen-Nation Disarmament Committee (ENDC). The US proposed that IAEA safeguards would apply to fissile material production and would include verification of continued shutdown of production facilities. Despite a lack of US initiative, the cut-off idea remained alive in the disarmament literature (Roberts 2001: 23).

Table 1. World Wide Nuclear Testing, 1945-2013

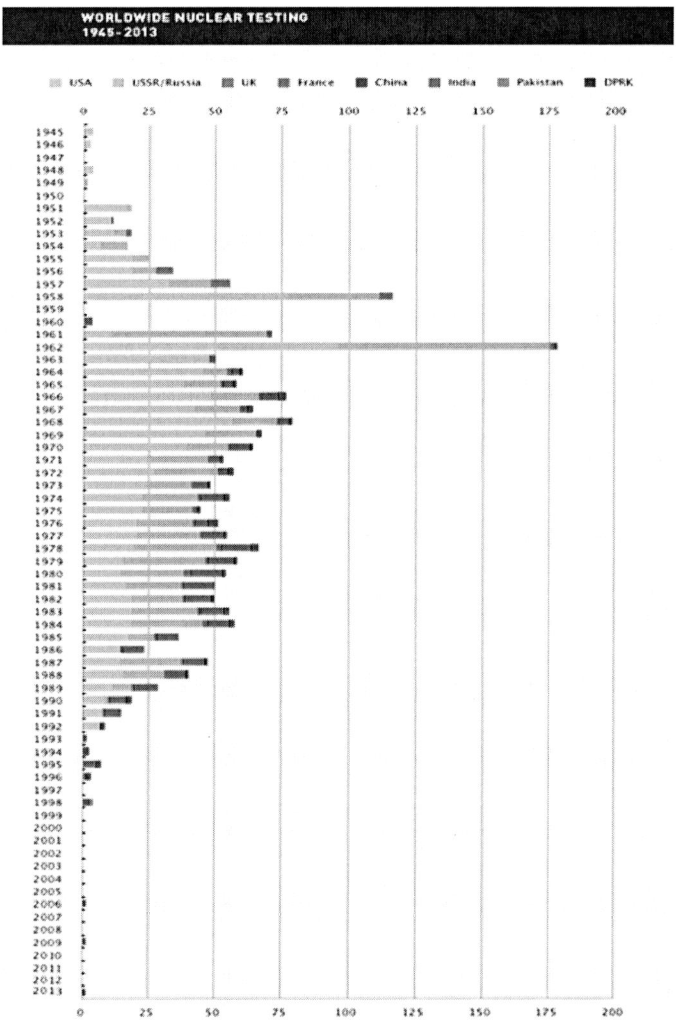

Source: *US Atomic Energy Commission, http://vrww.osti.gov/atomicenergyact.pdf.*

US Domestic Laws

The main pillars of the US nuclear non-proliferation policy consist of legislations that define the US commitment to the non-proliferation regime and provide enforcement and oversight mechanisms for its implementation (Davis and Donelly 1990). Nikitin, Mary Beth, Paul K. Kerr, Steven A. Hildreth (2012) pointed out the three main legislative pillars of US nuclear non-proliferation were the Atomic Energy Act (1954) asamended, the Nuclear Non-Proliferation Act (1978), and the Arms Export Control Act(1976).

Atomic Energy Act: It provides legal and primary authority for the development and oversight of the US government's nuclear programs to the Atomic Energy Commission (AEC), now the Nuclear Regulatory Commission (NRC). In 1974, these duties were separated and shared between the NRC and the Department of Energy[1]. One main objective of the Act was to establish controls on the "export of nuclear materials, goods, information, and technology." Under the Act, for exports of sensitive US nuclear technology to a foreign country the precondition is that the State Department must negotiate an agreement for nuclear cooperation. "Each agreement must meet several standards outlined in the IAEA" (Nikitin*et al.* 2012: 21). Countries that violate the terms of nuclear agreements with the US are given penalties and restrictions under the Act. Congress reviews all such protocols before they can come intoeffect.

Nuclear Non-Proliferation Act (NNPA): The NNPA adapted the dual role played internationally by the IAEA to US nuclear export policy. The NNPA intended to clarify and strengthen the US role as a reliable supplier of nuclear technology and nuclear fuels. The maintenance of US leadership and control over the international nuclear fuel cycle was seen as an effective tool "for restraining the spread of uraniumen richment and plutonium reprocessing facilities throughout the world. The NNPA further specified legal guidelines for the regulation of nuclear commerce and technical assistance by the US government"(CRS Report 1991). The Act requires recipient nations to accept full-scope safeguards on imports of US nuclear technology and materials. These requirements create incentives for cooperation with US nuclear non-proliferation policy (USNRC 2013: 1073).

Squassoni (2008) argued that NNPA was an attempt to revive the previous US objective to internationalize the fuel cycle by making international fuel cycle a fundamentally "less attractive platform from which to develop nuclear weapons." Section 309(c) of the NNPA directs the President to enact procedures to control US exports "which could be, if used for purposes other than those for which the export is intended, of significance for nuclear explosive purposes." Section 309(c) establishes jurisdiction over nuclear exports for the Departments of Commerce, State, Energy, Defense, and Arms Control and Disarmament Agency. Section 601 requires the President to report annually to the Congress on the Government's efforts to prevent nuclear proliferation.

Arms Export Control Act (AECA): The AECA was enacted on June 30, 1976. It "authorizes US government military sales, loans, leases, financing, and licensing of commercial arms sales to other countries" (Nikitin*et al.* 2012: 22). The AECA, together with the United States government, coordinates keeping into consideration key foreign policy issues such as non-proliferation and determines the eligibility for military sales, loans. "Section *3(f) (22 USC. 2753(f)* prohibits any country from military sales or leases if the United States' President determines that the country violates any binding commitments to the US under international treaties or agreements on non-proliferation or special nuclear materials" (CRS Report for Congress 1997). Section *40 (22 USC. 2780)* prohibits exports or assistance in exporting (financial or otherwise) munitions to countries that provide support for terrorism. Terrorist acts are defined as activities that "aid or abet the international proliferation of nuclear explosive devices" to individuals or groups.

Section *101 (22 USC. 2799aa)* (previously Section 669 of the Foreign Assistance Act) "prohibits foreign economic or military assistance to countries that deliver or receive nuclear enrichment equipment, materials, or technology unless the supplier agrees to place such under safeguards and the recipient has full-scope safeguards. The President has the authority to waive sanctions in the interests of vital US national interests with an assurance that the recipient country will not acquire, develop, or assist others in acquiring or developing nuclear weapons" (CRS Report for Congress 1997). Section *102 (22 USC. 2799aa-1)* (previously Section 670 of the Foreign Assistance Act) prohibits foreign economic or military assistance to countries that deliver or receive nuclear processing equipment, material, or technology to or from another country; or any non-nuclear weapons state that could contribute to nuclear proliferation. Here also the President has the authority to waive the sanction.

The Nuclear Non-proliferation Act, discussed below, incorporated, through the AECA in 1994, the Glenn-Symington (1977) amendments on enrichment and reprocessing and the Pressler Amendment (1985) which was found in the Foreign Assistance Act, as amended (1961). The Pressler amendment conditioned aid to Pakistan on a written Presidential determination to the Congress that "Pakistan does not possess a nuclear explosive device and that the proposed United States assistance program will reduce significantly the risk that Pakistan will possess a nuclear explosive device"(Nikitin *et al.* 2012:23).

Other domestic laws reinforce the three main legislations. The Export Administration Act (EEA), 1979 (PL 96-72) authorizes the President to regulate the private sector exports of certain materials and technology to other countries. Although the Act expired in 2001, export controls have been implemented under executive orders and the *International Emergency Economic PowersAct (IEEPA)*. The "Export-Import Bank Act of 1945 (PL 79-173) authorizes the Bank to finance and facilitate exports and imports and the exchange of commodities and services between the United States and other countries." It authorizes to deny credit to any person or country if the person or the country does not help in advancing US non-proliferation policy (Nikitin*et al.* 2012:23).

Besides, the US has laws to deal with specific concerns about a particular country or countries. The *Nunn-Lugar/ Cooperative Threat Reduction Program Legislation* which came to be named as Nunn-Lugar Amendment of 1991 established programs by the Congress to assist Russia to keep nuclear weapons safe, secure and help in dismantling nuclear weapons in Russia and other satellite states of the former Soviet Union. It was expanded to include various proliferation risks from weak political control over nuclear materials, facilities, equipment together with chemical and biological weapons and missiles. Specific Acts such as Iran-Iraq Arms Nonproliferation Act (1992) oppose any transfer to Iran or Iraq that could contribute to either country's ability to acquire nuclear, chemical, biological, or advanced conventional weapons. The Iran, North Korea and Syria Nonproliferation Act (1992) target these countries by imposing penalties and sanctions to transfer or receive from any of the three countries that could violate international non-proliferation treaties or agreements (Squassoni 2008).

Moreover, the Departments of State, Energy, Defense, Treasury, and Commerce, and the intelligence community are all involved in the formulation and implementation of the non-proliferation policy. Congress mandated the creation of a White House Coordinator for the Prevention of Weapons of Mass Destruction Proliferation and Terrorism (PL 110-53) (Nikitin*etal.* 2012:19). The US Department of Energy (DOE), for example, provided ample support to the US non-proliferation efforts through its *Co-operative Threat Reduction (CTR) Program*. The CTR helped the former Soviet states to dismantle many nuclear facilities and materials. Since then, the United States and Russia have been cooperating, through several programs, to secure and eliminate many of the materials so that terrorists or rogue nations could not acquire any nuclear weapon or explosive capabilities.

International Treaties/Agreements

Besides an array of domestic legislations to prevent nuclear proliferation, the US has played an active part in the creation of multilateral institutions aimed at the same goal. The NPT is the central focus of nuclear non-proliferation efforts. Other treaties include the Convention on the Physical Protection of Nuclear Material, International Convention for the Suppression of Acts of Nuclear Terrorism, Comprehensive Nuclear Test Ban Treaty (CTBT) and regional nuclear-weapon-free zones. In addition to these multilateral treaties, the United States has also initiated multilateral initiatives such as G-8 Global Partnership to Combat WMD, Proliferation Security Initiative (PSI) and bilateral agreements with specific countries to deal with the menace of nuclear proliferation and its dangers (Nikitin *et al.*2012:9).

In 1963, the US, along with the former Soviet Union and Great Britain, signed the Limited Test Ban Treaty(LTBT)[2] that prohibited nuclear testing in the atmosphere, outer space, and underwater. China and France refused to sign, and both the superpowers continued their quests for maintaining nuclear superiority. Although it did not produce any substantial result, it was the first agreement and an important precedent towards arms control and nuclear disarmament. However, thistreaty could not bring the desired result of terminating all nuclear tests. To a certainextent, such steps were regarded as steps to encourage countries not to follow the nuclear path (Halloway 2010).

I. Treaty on the Non-Proliferation of Nuclear Weapons

China's nuclear detonation in 1964 irked the US in particular and the international community in general. It happened within two years after President Kennedy echoed his fear of a possibility of the US facing "a world in which fifteen or twenty or twenty-five nations may have these weapons" (Simpson 1985). The US was stepping up its diplomatic activity to prevent any such test and proliferation which ultimately led to the signing of the multilateral treaty–Treaty on the Non-Proliferation of Nuclear Weapons commonly known as the Nuclear Non-Proliferation Treaty (NPT). The basis of the NPT (the central bargain) was to forbid Nuclear Weapon States (NWS) to assist any other nation in acquiring nuclear weapons. At the same time, the Non-Nuclear Weapons Weapon States (NNWS) committed themselves not to acquire any nuclear weapons capability.[3] It creates an overt international rule that NNWS should not seek nuclear weapons.

The treaty was signed in July 1968 and came intoforce on March 5, 1970. However, the treaty was criticized as discriminatory for its distinction between nuclear "haves" and "have-nots" (Simpson 1985). Many non-nuclear-weapon states claims that while insisting on non-nuclear-weapon states never to acquire nuclear weapons, the nuclear-weapon states, have not been able to fulfil the disarmament commitments in NPT which was the basis of the "central bargain" in NPT negotiations. The nuclear "have-nots" point to the failure by the nuclear "haves", particularly the United States, for its failure to ratify the CTBT which would ban all forms of nuclear testing (Grahams 2004). After the NPT was in place, the N-5 "showed no interest in fulfilling their part of the bargain", particularly, the pledge for nuclear disarmament envisaged in Article VI of the NPT (Udgoankar

1999: 159). NPT was made a permanent treaty in 1995 by member-states. Member states agreed on a more robust review process at a Review Conference in May 2010, to make the treaty stronger and enable the IAEA to pursue the responsibility of verification and ensure compliance by member states with "nuclear safeguard measures."

The US Department of State (2013) stated that many countries had the potential to develop nuclear weapons in the 1960s. The "spread of nuclear weapons technology was a chief motivator as well as a fear among the nuclear haves." The doctrine of nuclear deterrence was meaningful for the United States, its closest ally Britain, and the former Soviet Union as they had enough nuclear weapons' stockpiles in their silos. However, the horizontal proliferation of nuclear weapons, particularly, acquiring nuclear weapons by developing countries, if it happened, was a threat to the system of balance of power or deterrence that existed between the two Cold War rival camps. The United States and Britain were clubbed on one side and the former Soviet Union on the other side of the rival camps. This fissure also caused the nuclear states to hesitate in sharing nuclear technology with the developingcountries. Allofthese concerns led to international interest in a nuclear non-proliferation treaty that would help prevent the spread of nuclear weapons.

Jonas (2006) argued that there were challenges put up by developing countries about their reluctance to fall in line to give up any intension of developing or acquiring nuclear weapons. Finally, the NPT was signed by making many non-nuclear-weapon states to sign through persuasion. The final treaty includes all clauses aimed at limiting the spread of nuclear weapons and technology. The central bargain was clear – "the NPT non-nuclear-weapon states agree never to acquire nuclear weapons and the NPT nuclear-weapon states in exchange agree to share the benefits of peaceful nuclear technology and to pursue nuclear disarmament aimed at the ultimate elimination of their nuclear arsenals" (Graham 2004). All the signatories agreed to submit to the safeguards against proliferation provision established by the International Atomic Energy Agency(IAEA)[4].

The Nuclear Non-proliferation Treaty was to become "the most successful and widely subscribed arms control treaty in history, with 188 states parties" (Jonas 2006: 607-608). During the negotiations on the NPT, the proposal for a ban on the production of fissile materials was placed, along with a host of other measures, including negotiations on a comprehensive nuclear test ban treaty (Jonas 2006: 608). However, its success is limited. Israel, India, and Pakistan acquired nuclear weapons and became de-facto nuclear weapon states soon instead. Moreover, North Korea withdrew from the NPT and tested its nuclear weapons in 2006, 2009 and 2011, respectively.

The UN claims NPT is the "only binding commitment in a multilateral treaty to the goal of disarmament by the nuclear-weapons States" (UNODA, 2019). However, NPT has not been able to prevent countries from availing nuclear technologies and building nuclear weapons. The current four de-facto states viz. India, Pakistan, North Korea, and Israel are out of this treaty. Even two of the nuclear-weapon states (China and France) have not ratified the NPT and are only in acceding stage or parties to the treaty (UNODA 2014). There are a few challenges to the current NPT regime: challenge from the de-facto nuclear weapon states; challenge from within the NPT by North Korea[5] and Iran; challenge from below in the form of nuclear trafficking and terrorism; and challenge from above by the five declared nuclear-weapons states (Njolstad 2011). A similar argument on the challenge to the NPT regime from within has been argued by Graham (2004). He wrote that, from within, Iran, Iraq and North Korea had threatened the NPT.

Nikitin *et al.* (2012) argued that the non-proliferation regime has not stopped all proliferation. However, it has helped in many ways in restraining nuclear flow, restrict development ambitions, and reinforcing "international norm of behavior" strongly condemning proliferation. He further argued that many countries like Argentina, Brazil, South Africa, Iraq, Taiwan, Sweden, and South Korea had developed sufficient nuclear weapons capability to acquire nuclear weapons at one time or another but did not pursue. Argentina, Brazil, South Korea, Sweden, Taiwan, and South Africa[6] abandoned their nuclear weapons programs and joined the NPT as non-nuclear-weapons states. Libya gave up its clan destine nuclear weapons programs in December 2003.

The US Department of State (2013) stated that the US government saw the NPT "as a political and legal cornerstone of the nuclear non-proliferation regime as well as the basis for international cooperation on stemming the spread of nuclear weapons."In Prague on April 5, 2009, President Barack Obama put the US perspective of NPT when he said that the basic bargain at the core of the Treaty is sound: "countries with nuclear weapons will move towards disarmament; countries without nuclear weapons will not acquire them; and all countries can access peaceful nuclear energy."

II. Convention on the Physical Protection of Nuclear Material (CPPNM), and its Amendment

The Convention on the Physical Protection of Nuclear Material, originally entered into force in 1987, sets international standards for nuclear trade and commerce. The Convention outlines security requirements to protect nuclear materials from terrorist groups. The entry into force of the CPPNM and its Amendment were significant achievements in the development of the international legal framework for nuclear security. Till October 2018, 157 members were party to the treaty and forty-four were signatories according to the IAEA. Parties to the Convention agreed to report on the disposition of nuclear materials transported and IAEA assists and provides security in transportation. The United States is a strong advocate for in vigorating the treaty by extending controls to domestic facility security too. In 2005, the parties to the treaty convened to extend its scope to cover not only nuclear material in transportation but also the protection of nuclear materials from sabotage. The US, however, has not submitted its instrument of ratification yet to help the Convention incorporate the proposed new rules which need to be ratified by two-thirds of the State Parties of the Convention. In 2007, President Bush put the Amendment to the Senate for its ratification. President Obama in 2011 had also submitted draft legislation to the Senate, but no action was taken in the 112th Congress of the United States of America (Woolf *et al.* 2013:31).

III. Convention for the Suppression of Acts of Nuclear Terrorism

The International Convention for the Suppression of Acts of Nuclear Terrorism (also known as the Nuclear Terrorism Convention) was adopted by the United Nations General Assembly in 2005 after eight years of debating a draft treaty proposed by Russia in 1997. After the 9/11 terrorist attacks on the US, many countries revisited for the draft treaty, and the earlier disputes on the definition of "terrorism" were resolved through necessary compromises. The treaty came into force in July 2007. Till February 2021, there were 117 state parties and 115 signatories. The United States strongly supported the Convention, and President George W. Bush signed it after Russia did. However, the US has not submitted the required instrument of ratification to the Convention. It commits each party to adopt measures in its national law to criminalize unlawful possession and use of radioactive or nuclear material or devices and also use or damage to nuclear facilities and make them punishable. It also commits state-parties to commit themselves in exchanging information and cooperation to "detect, prevent, suppress and investigate" those suspected of committing nuclear terrorism, including extraditions. However, the Convention applies to acts of individuals and not states. Hence, it does not cover armed forces' actions of a particular state/country in an armed conflict. The Convention also does not address "the issue of legality of the use or threat of use of nuclear weapons by States" (Woolf *et al.* 2013:32).

IV. Comprehensive Test Ban Treaty (CTBT),1996

Linking a nuclear test ban with nuclear non-proliferation, Epstein (1990) wrotetha the interpretation of NPT's Article VI connoted measures for a Comprehensive Test Ban (CTB). That is a ban on the production of fissile materials for weapons, a freeze on the production of nuclear weapons and aban on the flight testing of delivery vehicles. The Comprehensive Test Ban Treaty (CTBT) would ban all nuclear explosions. Parties to the treaty agreed "not to carry out any nuclear weapon test explosion or any other nuclear explosion" (Medalia 1998). It was opened for signatures in 1996 but did not enter into force. Previous treaties have restricted nuclear testing in space, atmosphere, underwater and underground explosions. President Clinton signed the CTBT in 1996, but the Senate rejected it in 1999. The treaty established a *Comprehensive Nuclear-Test-Ban Treaty Organization* (CTBTO) of all member states to implement the treaty.

The CTBTO oversees a Conference of States Parties. The CTBTO would come into effect if the treaty entered into force; until then the CTBTO Preparatory Commission conducts work to prepare for entry into force, such as building and operating the International Monitoring System (IMS). As of September 2019, 184 nations had signed the CTBT and 168 had ratified it. Of the 44 required nations, 36 have ratified, three have not signed (India, North Korea, and Pakistan) and another five have not ratified (China, Egypt, Iran, Israel, and the United States). Every two years, states that have ratified the CTBT have been holding Conferences since 1999 to accelerate the process of entering into force (Woolf*etal.* 2013:33). President George W. Bush administration opposed the treaty ratification while continuing the moratorium on exploding more bombs that have been continuing since 1992. In contrast, President Obama had repeatedly expressed his support for CTBT ratification (Warren 2011).

CTBT supporters and opponents have their arguments as to why the US should or should not ratify the treaty and what impact it would have on the global non-proliferation efforts. Supporters such as the former Director of IAEA, Hans Blix, argued that if the US ratifies there would be domino-effect in other countries. He declared that US ratification of CTBT would make China follow suit. Its neighbor, India, would likely follow China's ratification; and Indian response would propel Pakistan to follow. Ultimately, Iran would complete the chain by seeking ratification. Hence it would be a good domino-effect. Conversely, the opponents believe that the overseas impact of US ratification would be "mild". While "domino-style" response from countries after Washington's ratification of the CTBT might be the outcome, even slow a domino-effect would not start if the United States do not ratify the CTBT (Horovitz and Golan-Vilella 2010:236).

V. Regional Nuclear-Weapon-Free-Zones(NWFZ)

Regional nuclear-weapon-free-zones address the problems of horizontal nuclear proliferation in the regional context, where nuclear competition between rival neighboring states in sensitive regions are present that could have global repercussions (Khan 1990: 45-53). Some states had concluded regional treaties to declare nuclear-weapon-free-zones. These regions are - Latin America, South-east

Asia, the South-Pacific, Africa and Central Asia. Each Nuclear-Weapon-Free-Zone (NWFZ) treaty have protocols for the five nuclear-weapon states to adhere. The United States has ratified the Latin America NWFZ (Treaty of Tlatelolco) protocols. The Obama administration submitted the protocols for the African and South Pacific zones to the Senate for advice and consent in May 2011. Talks continued with parties to the South-east Asian and Central Asian zones to resolve issues (Nikitin*et al.* 2012: 12). Table (2) below shows the overall picture of the treaties and US adherence to the NWFZ protocols.

President Obama administration did show a willingness to raise issues of differences with the South-east Asian nations and Central Asian nations to sign the protocols to those treaties. The Consultations with the South-east Asian counterparts started and are "reportedly" in continuation. Also, talks were under way to discuss the establishment of a Middle-East (West Asia) WMD-free zone (Woolf *et al.* 2013: 30).

Table 2. US Adherence to Nuclear-Weapon-Free Zone Protocols

Treaty	Year Treaty Opened for Signature/Entered into Force	Year United States Signed Protocols	Year United States Ratified Protocols
Treaty of Tlatelolco (Latin America)	1967/1969	Protocol I: 1977 Protocol II: 1968	Protocol I: 1981 Protocol II: 1971
Treaty on a Nuclear-Weapon-Free Zone in Central Asia	2006/2009	Not signed	Not ratified
Treaty of Rarotonga (South Pacific)	1985/1986	Protocol I, II & III: 1996	Not ratified, submitted to the Senate, May 2, 2011
Treaty of Pelindaba (Africa)	1996/2009	Protocols I & II: 1996	Not ratified, submitted to the Senate, May 2, 2011
Treaty of Bangkok (Southeast Asia)	1995/1997	Not signed	Not ratified

Source: *CRS Report RL33865 (2013) at www.crs.gov.*

G-8 Global Partnership Against the Spread of Weapons and Materials of Mass Destruction

In June 2002, the Group of Eight (the United States, Canada, the United Kingdom, France, Germany, Italy and Japan (G-7) plus Russia (G-8) formed the G-8 Global Partnership Against the Spread of Weapons and Materials of Mass Destruction. It is a global forum that came to its existence with the support of the United States. In early 2002 the United States proposed to the G-8 to expand its Co-operative Threat Reduction programs called "10 plus 10 over 10" which meant the other G-8 countries wouldadd$10 billion more over 10 years to the $10 billion the United States was already planning to spend on CRT[1] related programs. Woolf Amy*et al.* (2013) wrote that "by expanding the programs to include more donors, the participants would not only be able to increase their level of effort in Russia but might also be able to address potential proliferation problems in other nations."

At the 2002 Summit, the G-8 countries adopted principles to deny any access to WMD and its materials to terrorists. At present, there are thirty-one active members of the Global Partnership, which do not include China, India, Pakistan, Israel, and North Korea. President Obama held the Presidency in 2012, and his administration continued its policy of actively promoting the expansion of the Partnership to new countries to promote greater attention to nuclear and radiological security, bio-security, facilitation of the implementation of the UN Security Council Resolution 1540 (this is mentioned in the following section), etc.

Informal Co-operativeInitiatives

Besides these treaties and agreements, there are a few important informal co-operative initiatives taken up by the international community with active participation from the United States. Let us discuss them in brief before we come to the last section of this part.

President George W. Bush announced the Proliferation Security Initiative (PSI) in May 2003. It is primarily a diplomatic tool to gain support for "interdicting" shipments of weapons of mass destruction-related (WMD) equipment and materials. Through the PSI, the Bush administration sought to, Woolf Amy, F.*et al.*(2013) wrote, "create a web of counter-proliferation partnerships through which proliferators will have difficulty carrying out their trade on WMD and missile-related technology." He further wrote that "The states involved in PSI have agreed to review their national legal authorities for interdiction, provide consent for other states to board and search their flag vessels, and conclude ship-boarding agreements."It is a significant initiative that has enabled the United States to conclude many ship-boarding agreements with many key-states.

Global Threat Reduction Initiative(GTRI) was started in 2004 by the US Department of Energy; it bridges any cooperation gap between the United States and Russia in preventing any diversion of HEU and other materials for making nuclear weapons. Both the countries summoned a GTRI International Partners' Conference to get support for GTRI-related projects in September 2004 and ninety countries have reportedly fused the GTRI after its establishment.

Global Initiative to Combat Nuclear Terrorism (GICNT) has fashioned irreplaceable benefactions in invigorating global potential to detect, intercept, and respond to nuclear terrorism. Till 2020, 89 partner countries and six international organizations have contributed to this area by completing 65 activities under the GICNT aimed at building partners' capabilities. Its observers include the IAEA, European Union (EU), and a few others. The GICNT collaborative efforts already complement the progress made and "help advance critical elements addressed" in the past two Nuclear Security Summits in Washington (2010) and Seoul (2012) (US Department of State 2014).

Non-proliferation Regimes

The US Department of Commerce (2014), as well as the US Department of State (2014), stated that the regimes registered underneath made a structure for participating governments to fight problems multilaterally in connection with export control and WMD proliferation. Concomitantly, the regimes are far-reaching by paying attention to the imperative threats to security. Independently, it singles out discrete threats comprising of chemical and biological weapons (The Australia Group), nuclear weapons (Nuclear Suppliers Group), delivery systems (Missile Technology Control Regime), and conventional arms (The Wassenaar Arrangement).

Multilateral Nuclear Non-proliferation Export Control

Nuclear Suppliers Group (NSG): The NSG is an important cartel that contributes to the non-proliferation for nuclear and related exports. The group has 48 current participating member-states. Currently, it is chaired by Argentina (2022-23). These member-states have expanded the role of the NSG to ensure that there is no proliferation of nuclear weapons or other disruptive activities. It has expanded strictly export instructions for nuclear materials meant exclusively for peaceful uses. Such recommendations embody nuclear material, technology and equipment, which is regarded as dual-use.

Zangger Committee: The task of the 39-nation Nuclear Non-proliferation Treaty (NPT) Exporters (Zangger) Committee is to systematize execution of the NPT requirements to apply International Atomic Energy Agency (IAEA) safeguards to nuclear exports. It does so by preparing a list of equipment and materials that may only be exported if safeguards are applied to the recipient facility (called the "Trigger List" on account of stimulating the necessities for prophylactic).

Missile Technology Control Regime (MTCR): The United States has been a member of the MTCR since its inception in 1987 with the hope of curtailing the menace of the proliferation of Weapons of Mass Destruction (WMD) delivery systems. Specifically, the purpose of the 35-MTCR collaborators is to limit the proliferation of missiles, outright rocket systems, unmanned air vehicles, and related technology for those systems capable of carrying a 500-kilogram payload at least 300 kilometers, as well as systems planning for the delivery of armaments of widespread ruination. It obtains its objectives through export controls and licensing relative information exchange between members, and outreach to non-members.

Success and Failure of the United States Non-Proliferation Initiatives

Since the inception of the nuclear epoch, the fear of nuclear weapons' use led to the search for establishment of international control of atomic energy. During and after the end of the Second World War, the United States was eager to maintain its monopoly on nuclear-bomb and hence its monopoly on nuclear technology as well. However, by 1953 the then Soviet Union and Britain had already exploded bombs. Recognizing the exercise to monopolize nuclear weapons, materials, technology, and secrets futile, the United States under President Eisenhower launched a new initiative called *"Atoms for Peace"* in his speech to the United Nations inDecember1953. It had two twin goals accompanied, namely, nuclear disarmament and liberalizing the peaceful uses of nuclear energy for civilian purposes under the strict supervision of the newly created IAEA (Halloway 2011:151-164).

Holloway (2011) wrote that the Statute of the IAEA

that charged the agency with responsibility to ensure non-diversion of nuclear energy "in such a way to further military purposes" by a specific country did not commit states to refrain from acquiring nuclear weapons or conducting nuclear activities outside the IAEA control. This loophole was to be filled by the NPT which was inscribed in 1968 and became operative in 1970. He argued that the "double bargain" that appears in NPT Article VI was brought in at a much later stage during negotiations. It was a hard-earned outcome of the pressure created by eight non-aligned members of the Eighteen-Nation Disarmament Committee (ENDC) in Geneva.

The "double bargain" entrusted a "balance of obligations" to both "nuclear haves" and "non-nuclear haves." Accordingly, the nuclear-weapon states would strive for "negotiations in good faith on effective measures in connection with the cessation of the nuclear arms race at an early date and to nuclear disarmament, and on a treaty on general and complete disarmament within the stringent and efficient international jurisdiction"(UNODA,2013). The non-nuclear-weapon states would not take any step to have nuclear weapons or indulge in any nuclear activities other than for civilian purposes.

Halloway (2011) further argued that although the United States had been committing to stop or at least halt nuclear proliferation since the Second World War, its policy had been shifting without any concrete approach thereby only dealing with particular issues that came up. The Chinese nuclear explosion in October 1964, however, prompted President Lyndon B. Johnson to set up Gilpatric Committee[2] drawing focus on intensified efforts to prevent the spread of nuclear weapons. The Committee's report helped in moving the United States to a broader and coherent approach to nuclear arms control, which assumed very high priority the respective administrations of President Johnson and his successor President Richard Nixon. When the UnitedStates signed the NPT, it took seriously Article VI and the language usedinit. On the question of the United States' commitment to the two other goals in Article VI, that is, nuclear disarmament and a treaty on general and complete disarmament, Holloway (2011) argued that its stance was not clear since it did not pay any serious political attention because of its too far futuristic and idealistic nature.

Arms control talks between the two superpowers went hand in hand with disarmament. The Committee's report in January 1965 specifically pointed out the need to pursue arms control measures, lessened emphasis on nuclear weapons, and cessation of the nuclear arms race between the two superpowers if other countries are to be induced to abstain from acquiring nuclear weapons indefinitely. In the meeting between President Ronald Reagan and Soviet leader Mikhail Gorbachev in Reykjavik (Iceland) in October1986, the two leaders talked about deep cuts in nuclear arsenals. They reportedly talked briefly on the possibility of elimination of all nuclear warheads altogether by the two. American reactions from the strategic community and government officials were instructive (critical).

However, post-Reykjavik meeting, as Holloway (2011) put, there were cuts in nuclear weapons - drastically reduced from 76,000 in 1986 to 23,000 by 2010. The two superpowers also signed several arms control treaties including the INF Treaty in 1987, START I in 1991 and START II in 1993. The progress made in arms control was matched with the progress in nuclear non-proliferation. South Africa signed the NPT in 1991 by leaving out its nuclear weapons program. Belarus, Kazakhstan, and Ukraine signed the NPT in the 1990s. They took decisions not to possess the nuclear warheads that had been kept in their territory after the former Soviet Union was separated. The role of the United States in making this possible deserve big applause. The Clinton administration took further the goal of ensuring further reductions in nuclear forces and the strengthening of the non-proliferation regime. The indefinite extension of the NPT in 1995 and the negotiation of the CTBT in 1996 are reflective of the efforts.

After the IAEA discovered, after the first Gulf War, that Iraq had progressed towards building nuclear weapons, there was a sense of threats emerging from "rogue states" and non-state actors that could harm the interests of the United States and its allies. Iraq dismantled its nuclear program under the auspices of the IAEA. A *"Framework Agreement"* was negotiated in 1994 with North Korea afterit ended its cooperation with the IAEA and threatened to break-out from the NPT - a signatory then. The United States responded promptly before the negotiation. These were the two cases of countries that attempted to violate their commitments under NPT in favor of clandestine nuclear programs.

The international agency along with active support from the United States did prevent the two from acquiring nuclear weapons. However, later in 2006, North Korea succeeded in its attempt to acquire nuclear weapons by actually detonating a nuclear device. Before this India and Pakistan in May 1998 had conducted nuclear weapon tests. The George W. Bush administration introduced some episodic and remarkable innovations and measures such as Proliferation Security Initiative (PSI) - a counter-proliferation initiative through which shipment of weapons of mass destruction (WMD) could be interdicted through cooperation among states; and United Nations Security Council Resolution 1540 to invigorate the non-proliferation regime. Jonas (2006) claimed that direct government-to-government negotiations and pressure had brought some remarkable achievements like abstaining from Libya's nuclear program in 2003 and accession of all states separated from Soviet to the NPT as non-nuclear- weapon states. In the case of Libya, he argued, that it was because of Iraq-bombing by the Bush administration in 2003 that propelled Libyans to withdraw nuclear ambition.

Bunn (2003) observed the inconsistencies in the US position towards nuclear non-proliferation measures. For example, he stated that "the Bush administration had pressed hard on Iraq, Iran, and North Korea to restrain them from acquiring nuclear weapons, but it has done so sometimes in unilateral or domineering ways that seem inconsistent with a multilateral regime like that of the NPT." To gain the agreement of the non-nuclear-weapon NPT parties to the treaty's extension in 1995, the United States also pledged that it would not use nuclear weapons against non-nuclear-weapon NPT parties unless they attack the United States while in alliance with another nuclear-weapon state. However, in its Nuclear Posture Review of 2001, and its National Strategy on Weapons of Mass Destruction of 2002, President Bush administration opined that it was ready to use nuclear weapons against a non-nuclear-weapon NPT party. Thus, Schaper and Muller (2004), opined that the Bush administration's security strategy was based on "complete freedom of action", whereby the United States projects "absolute military superiority."

President Bush administration took many unilateral actions that contradicted the above initiatives. Some of the initiatives such as unilaterally abrogating the Anti-Ballistic Missile (ABM) Treaty; refusing to work for ratification of Comprehensive Test Ban Treaty (CTBT) which the US signed in 1996; rejection of the idea of a verifiable Fissile Material Cut-off Treaty (FMCT); and responding to the threats from "rogue states" and terrorist groups through "preemption" unilaterally, if required, effectively brought back the centrality of the threat of use of nuclear force in American national security policies. These were the main obstacles to the non-proliferation regime from outside the treaty and somehow a failure of the United States' and the international community's nuclear non-proliferation initiatives.

President Obama administration started with an all-encompassing positive speech in Prague (2009). In Prague he not only asserted US commitment to eliminate nuclear weapons but also listed few steps his administration would undertake: first, amove toward a nuclear-free world; second, to strengthen the NPT; and third, to ensure that nuclear weapons are safe from terrorist hands. The President also reiterated his commitment toward sratification of the CTBT, going for a verifiable FMCT treaty thereby bringing the centrality his commitment to bringing a nuclear-free world which brought out, in the forefront, the clarity of his vision on the question of the central bargain of the NPT.

However, non-proliferation as an international issue was rekindled and brought back to the international attention by President Obama's policy. A legal binding replacement agreement to the Strategic Arms Reduction Treaty (START) was signed between the United States and Russia. It got replaced by the New START, which made entry into force in February 2011. In 2010, as a result of Obama administration's insistence on strengthening nuclear non-proliferation, Washington Nuclear Security Summit (2010) did successfully concluded. The Obama administration had also pledged to win Senate ratification of the CTBT. The administration had reportedly started discussions with the Pentagon in connection with the potential deep cuts to the US nuclear arsenals(Councilon Foreign Relations 2013).

On September 24, 2009, President Obama chaired a UN Security Council Summit on nuclear disarmament and nuclear non-proliferation. It was the first in the history of the USA that a US President took as a chair in one of the Sessions of the UN Security Council. The Council unanimously adopted Resolution 1887, by demanding some accelerated attempts towards nuclear disarmament and laying down actions to accomplish the goal.

Holloway (2011) stated that President Obama set out his idea of a nuclear-weapons-free world. This was to be preceded by the strengthening of the non-proliferation regime through new institutions and mechanisms of enforcement that could create a global nuclear order whereby the violators would be severely punished to stop any repetition of such violation. He argued that nuclear weapons states "will get rid of their nuclear weapons only" if they were convinced that the non-proliferation regime could prevent states from breaking out and punish those that has attempted to do so. Thus, in a way, Halloway (2011) was advocating that nuclear disarmament should go hand in hand with nuclear non-proliferation.

Nevertheless, there is a question about this. The question is, what would happen if the desired nuclear order does not emerge. This issue is important and likely to be effected by the way crises over Iran and North Korea are resolved. In February 2013, North Korea tested its third nuclear test despite the United States-led *Six-Party Talks* on North Korea trying to resolve the North Korean crisis. Iran's talks with the United States-led *P5+1* bore fruit during the Obama administration, and it kind led hope of a nuclear-free Iran until the Trump administration withdrew from the deal, thereby making Iran isolated again.

According to the *Stockholm International Peace Research Institute's* (SIPRI) yearbook (2013), all five nuclear weapons states were either deploying new nuclear weapons or delivery systems for nuclear systems or plans to do so. It specified that the five recognized weapons states appeared to retain their nuclear arsenals indefinitely, which was against the central bargain of the NPT by which they were supposed to commit themselves towards nuclear disarmament. The report still holds even today.

There are domestic and international reasons behind the success and failure of the United States initiatives for non-proliferation. The nuclear proliferation's problem is global, and it certainly needs international co-operative efforts – something the Obama administration did acknowledge. The domestic factor revolves around debates within the United States on nuclear disarmament. The US policy on nuclear proliferation requires a high-performance rate as it is often linked to revealing a government's abilities and limitations. External environment and responses from the allies and more extensive international community on nuclear proliferation complement the US thinking and strategy to deal with the menace of nuclear proliferation.

Domestic Factors

Assessment of the US nuclear non-proliferation policy until the late 1970s by Brenner (1981) reflected critical view. He wrote that general failings of US policy had been ones of "inadequacy" and "mistiming", that is lack of foresight, one-dimensional planning, poor coordination and general characteristic weakness of diplomatic initiatives. He argued that the United States government displayed "a failure to provide clear and continuous political guidance to its international program for supporting the civilian use of nuclear power." For example, he wrote that official policy moved between the range of "highly restrictive approach" taken by the Atomic Energy Act of 1946 as well as the "generous" and "tolerant" attitude of the Atoms for Peace program.

Holloway (2011) summed up the contemporary debate in the US, which has shaped the current American thinking and US policy to an extent. He has pointed out three main issues in the debate. The first issue was on the desirability of a world free from nuclear weapons. Supporters of the vision were widespread but not universal, he argued. Supporters argued that it would make the world more peaceful and stable. The world would be no more gripped with fear of a nuclear war between or among nations that was the phenomenon during the Cold War years. Its critics argued that nuclear weapons hadhelped prevent wars. It hadhelped in deterrence, and hence nuclear weapons were a stabilizing force and preferable. The second issue wasabout feasibility. The opponents of the vision of a nuclear-weapon-free world claimedthat such a world was not feasible. Hence, it would be better to focus on how to manage international control of nuclearweapons through monitoring measures and verification mechanisms. Supporters of nuclear disarmament argued that it provided an essential guide to the journey towards a safer and more secure nuclear order.

The third issue was a crucial one which was the connectionbetween disarmament and nuclear non-proliferation. One argument was that disarmament led to proliferation. One example cited to explain this was that during the Cold War, the US nuclear umbrella to its allies during Cold War led to halting of the spread of nuclear weapons during the time of the Cold War. If the US had to move towards utter destruction of nuclear weapons, some of the beneficiaries of the extended deterrence might seek nuclear options for themselves. The other argument was that determined states such as India, Pakistan, North Korea and Israel haddefied all sanctions and possible actions against them to acquire nuclear weapons on their own. They did when they felt that they needed them and would do so in the future as well. Nevertheless, frankly speaking, the link between nuclear disarmament and non-proliferation was well tested during the Obama administration, which has been analyzed above.

The disagreement on the feasibility of a nuclear-weapons-free world in Congress was sharp. In 2008,

Congress set up the Commission on the Strategic Posture of the United States to help guide the Next Nuclear Posture. The Commission had six Democrats and six Republicans with William J. Perry[3] (former Secretary of Defense) as the Chairman and James Schlesinger (an ardent critic of the notion of a world, non-existence of nuclear weapons) as the Vice-Chairman. The Commission's Report stated the "differences over whether the conditions can ever be created that might enable the elimination of nuclear weapons" (United States Institute of Peace 2009). Also, factors such as the refusal of the United States Senate to ratify even after President Obama attempted to win for ratification, US proposed modernization of nuclear weapons, gave an impression to other countries that all that the President proclaimedwere reflective of US nuclear policy rhetoric which had strong elements to bully other countries (Becker 2013).

Contrary to what President Barack Obama's commitment to nucleard is armament, a Congressional Budget Office(CBO) report proposed that the US government spent $355 billion over the next ten years to upgrade and develop a new generation of nuclear weapons. This was "nearly $150 billion more than the administration's $208.5 billion estimates to Congress last year." Besides, the Obama administration's review called for more investment "to restore and modernize the national laboratories and the complex of supporting facilities that maintain the nation's nuclear weapons stockpile. The costs of those modernization activities will add significantly to the overall cost of the nation's nuclear forces, which also includes the cost of operating and maintaining the current forces" (Congressional Budget Office (CBO)2013).

External Factors

A world free of nuclear weapons would be of great interest to the United States since it would remove all of what the United States was worried about – a nuclear attack on the United States by a "rogue state" or a terrorist group (Council on Foreign Affairs 2014). As mentioned, global nuclear proliferation is a global phenomenon, and it needs international cooperation. However, international cooperation will be complicated by a number of factors. According to a CRS Report (1991), "The difficulties the United States is having maintaining the cooperation of member countries in regimes are examples of the new types of challenges facing the US non-proliferation policy. New and more refined methods of persuasion and consensus-building may be required to sustain the non-proliferation regimes"(CRS Report 1991).

First, although the United States put the concern of nuclear proliferation and nuclear terrorism at the top of the priority list, not all nuclear powers give them the topmost priority. Second, a major power like Russia still uses the nuclear option to deter traditional attacks. The most recent example is Russia's empty threat to use nuclear weapons against adversaries during its war on Ukraine. It fears that elimination of nuclear weapons would turn Russia into a vulnerable state, having chances of being coerced by a superior conventional force like that of the United States'. Third, most of the nuclear powers (including de facto powers such as India, Pakistan, Israel and North Korea) link their nuclear weapons with survival and broader security concerns. Furthermore, this makes them highly unlikely to pay much attention to the call for a nuclear-weapons-free world. Oppositions of nuclear disarmament suggest that it would make more beneficial and gaining tasks to the proliferators like Iran without losing anything in obtaining nuclear weapons. These differences would complicate the effort to make progress towards a world free of nuclear weapons (Holloway 2011: 150-166).

The United States has not kept the non-proliferation issue as the priority in its foreign and national security policy. It might not be in the future too. Otherstrategicand economic interests have, at times, prevailed over non-proliferation considerations. For example, under the provisions of the *Pressler Amendment,* President Ronald Reagan submitted annual written determinations to Congress that "Pakistan does not possess a nuclear explosive device and that the proposed United States assistance program will reduce significantly the risk that Pakistan will possess a nuclear explosive device" *(CRS 7 Report, 1991)* for the years 1985 through 1988. In 2006, the United States signed the Indo-US Civil Nuclear deal thereby exempting India from the NSG waiver and put India as an exceptional non-NPT state which could have nuclear trade and commerce with the international community. The United States seems to have various foreign policies and security aims willingly and intentionally subordinate to non-proliferation goals. For this reason, other countries would have the desire to make an international consensus against proliferation.

There are obstacles, both domestic and international, that create a barrier in the way of nuclear disarmament. Itis to be acknowledged. However, it would be better not to focus on obstacles alone. The "double bargain, which represents the central bargain of the nuclear proliferation regime should be pursued vigorously and sincerely. Indeed, President Obama had opened for the United States a large window to invite serious discussions and creative efforts to resolve the danger of nuclear weapons.

The CRS Report of 1991 stated that "to slow the expansion of the raw materials of mass destruction is to have some sacrifice." Ultimately, the US could opt to strengthen the regimes it was instrumental in creating, orto allow them to erode, or to maintain them at their present levels. The United States cannot afford to lose focus on the emphasis of creating a safe and secure world order free from nuclear dangers while pursuing other vital strategic and economic interests of the United States. The nuclear disarmament effort revived by the Obama administration is to be further channelized and give a new impetus. Fissile Material Cut-off Treaty(FMCT) presents the next multilateral challenge towards nuclear disarmament about which, the next chapter has discussed in detail.

Notes

1. The Energy Reorganization Act of 1974 abolished the AEC and divided its responsibilities between the Nuclear Regulatory Commission, which oversees and regulates civilian and commercial aspects of atomic energy, and the Department of Energy, which operates the nuclear research laboratories and the nuclear weapons complex.
2. The Limited Test Ban Treaty (LTBT) aimed at reducing conventional forces and armaments together with eliminating nuclear weapons. In this sense, many scholars believe it is an arms control treaty, not a nuclear-non-proliferation treaty. However, the United Nations Office for Disarmament Affairs (UNODA) (2013) stated that it was one of the multilateral treaties established "with the aim of preventing nuclear proliferation and testing, while promoting progress in nuclear disarmament." Thus, it is undercontention. See,*URL:http://www.un.org/disarmament/WMD/Nuclear/.*
3. NPT Article I and II.
4. The IAEA was established after the "Atoms for Peace"proposal in the UNGA in 1953 by President Eisenhower. It was established in 1956 and went into formal operation in 1957.
5. It withdrew from NPT in January 2003. Singal (2011) opinedthat it was imperative to understand critically as to why North Korea defected from NPT. He refuted the prevailing view that it did so because it considered itself

destined to arm. Rather, he argued that North Korea's sense of "insecurity"with the US' hostile policy toward it together

With an urge to forge new (fundamentally changed) relationships with the US, Japan and South Korea explained its nuclear policy of retaining a nuclear option and hence its withdrawal from the NPT. Thus, Njolstad (2011) opined that bringing North Korea back into the NPT was itself a challenge to the NPT regime. This challenge, he thought, was from within the NPT regime given that North Korea was a signatory toNPT.

6. was the only country in this group to have built and abandoned actual warheads. Ukraine, Kazakhstan, and Belarus returned nuclear weapons inherited from the former Soviet Union to Russia and opted to join the NPT as non-nuclear-weapons states.

7. Co-operative Threat Reduction (CTR) programis administered bythe US Department of Defense, US Department of State and US Department of Energy. Funded by Congress, the CTR program aimed to assist Russia, Ukraine, Belarus, and Kazakhstanconcerning the handling of nuclear weapons, its storage, safe and secure transportation and dismantling of nuclear weapons previously under the custody of the former Soviet Union. The first few years the United States had a mandate of providing "assistance to materials that might be used in nuclear or chemical weapons" to prevent any diversion of technical know-how from the former Soviet Union and to assist in demilitarization efforts of defense industries in the former Soviet Union republics, etc. (Woolf et al. 2013). The CTR mandate now expands beyond the former Soviet Republics and includes "willing countries" to reduce the threats from Weapons of Mass Destruction (WMDs) and relatedmaterials,technologiesandexpertise.See,URL:*http://comptroller.defense.gov/Portals/45/Documents/defbudget/fy2014/budget_justification/pdf/01_Operation_and_Maintenance/*

O_M_VOL_1_PART_2/CTR_OP-5.pdf.

8. Under former Deputy Secretary of Defense Roswell Gilpatric. The purpose was to study the problem of nuclear proliferation

9. Along with George Schultz (President Reagan's Secretary of State), Sam Nunn (former Senator), and Henry Kissinger (former Secretary of State). They were known as the "Gang of Four," the "Four Horsemen," or the "Quartet." They attended a Conference in October 2006 organized by the Hoover Institution at Stanford University to mark the 20th anniversary of Reykjavik summit meeting between President Ronald Ragan and Premier Mikhail Gorbachev in 1986. The most important result of the Conference was an article in the Wall Street Journal in January 2007, where four signed the article calling for a world free of nuclear weapons. The op-edpieces high-profile authorship helped shift the debate within the US government and other policy circles. President Obama had endorsed this perspective calling for the same vision of a nuclear-weapons-free world. In 1987, ironically, Kissinger and Richard Nixon criticized Reagan when both the leaders of the two superpowers in Reykjavik floated the possibility of having a nuclear weapons-free world.

3

US Position on FMCT: Role of Domestic Factors

Introduction

The previous chapter has dealt with the detail the United States' approach to nuclear non-proliferation initiatives. It has been argued that the Obama administration supported an initiative toward global nuclear non-proliferation. President Obama's proposed nuclear disarmament agenda conformed to the administration's stand on the need for the conclusion of a Fissile Material Cutoff Treaty (FMCT). In this context, as mentioned in the previous chapter, the current US administration sees an effective and verifiable FMCT as a stepping stone towards the goal of a nuclear-weapons-free world. Why is it important for the US to have an effective and verifiable cut-off treaty? How seriously does the US pursue it? What are the domestic factors that govern the current US position on FMCT? These are some crucial questions that are worth examining and analyzing in order to understand the underlying US position on FMCT.

The chapter starts by defining fissile material – the main subject of the FMCT. This is essential to give abroad idea on the desirability or rather essentiality of concluding an FMCT in the Conference on Disarmament (CD). The chapter is divided into two sections. The first section has discussed how the negotiations for FMCT have evolved. It traces and analyzes its origin and subsequent developments to make it more coherent and comprehensive. It has also examined and analyzed fissile material negotiations in the Conference on Disarmament (CD), besides bringingout the significance of an FMCT. The second section has dealt with the US position on the FMCT and the role of American domestic factors.

Fissile Material

Acquiring fissile material is considered by most non-proliferation experts as the main hurdle in developing nuclear weapons. Fissile materials such as plutonium-239 (Pu-239), uranium-233 (U-233), and uranium enriched in the isotope uranium-235 (U-235) are produced in several ways. The isotope U-235 occurs naturally but not in abundance (only0.7 % of the natural uranium). However, a nuclear bomb can only be made from concentrated uranium in a significant amount. It suggests that U-235 is to be concentrated through an advanced process separately. High-enriched uranium (HEU) is produced by concentrating the isotope U-235 in an enrichment plant[1] Pu-239 is created in a nuclear reactor by irradiating predominant natural uranium (U-238) (99.3% of the natural uranium). "The Pu-239 is then chemically separated from the highly radioactive fission products[2] to be usable in a nuclear weapon. U-233 is produced in a reactorby irradiating thorium-232, and also requires chemical separation from fission products" (CRS Report Squassoni, *et al.* 2006:2).

The International Atomic Energy Agency (IAEA) Statute defines "special fissionable materials" as plutonium-239; uranium-233; uranium enriched in the isotopes 235 or 233 "which means uranium containing the isotopes 235 or

233 or both in an amount such that the abundance ratio of the sum of these isotopes to the isotope 238 is greater than the ratio of the isotope 235 to the isotope 238 occurring in nature" (Sethi 1998:1381).

The US White Paper on a Fissile Material Cut-off Treaty (2006) proposed by the George W. Bush administration defined fissile material as "Pu except for Pu where the isotopic composition includes 80% or greater Pu-238 and uranium containing 20% or greater enrichment in U-233 or U-235." The US Nuclear Regulatory Commission (US NRC) (2013) identified three primary fissile materials:uranium-233, uranium-235, and plutonium-239. The definition of the US NRC excluded non-irradiated natural uranium and depleted uranium, or "that have not been irradiated in thermal reactors."

Road to FMCT

The significant development in FMCT occurred in 1978. A Canadian Proposal in the Tenth Special Session of the UN devoted to 'disarmament' called for banning the fissile materials for use in weapons in order to "suffocate" nuclear proliferation. In 1979, the United Nations established the Conference on Disarmament (CD) as the single permanent multilateral disarmament negotiating platform for theso-called "international community"[3]. Beginning with a membership of only forty members, the CD now comprises sixty-five member-states[4]. It is the successor to theTen-Nation Committee on Disarmament (1960), the Eighteen-Nation Disarmament Committee (1962-1968), and the Conference on the Committee on Disarmament (1969-1978). It was generally understood that the Cold War made an FMCT impractical and blocked any possible progress as the two superpower rivals were reluctant to reduce their stockpiles at a level lower than the irrivals(Stevens1999).

The key event that propelled the FMCT into the

limelight was President Bill Clinton's address to the United Nations in 1993[5], wherein he stated that the United States.

> "will pursue new steps to control the materials for nuclear weapons. Growing global stockpiles of plutonium and highly enriched uranium are raising the danger of nuclear terrorism for all nations." Moreover, it continued, the United States would press for an international agreement that would ban the production of these materials for weapons forever"(US Department of State1993).

In September 1993, President Clinton proposed a framework in the UN General Assembly (UNGA) that included a proposed multilateral convention prohibiting the production of fissile materials (plutonium and highly enriched uranium) for nuclear weapons and devices and put such materials under international safeguards which the UNGA soon adopted. After that, it has been referred to informally as the FMCT.

In response to UN General Assembly Resolution 48/75L[6], in December 1993, the UNGA passed Resolution 48/75L entitled, "Prohibition of Production of Fissile Material for Nuclear Weapons or Other Nuclear Explosive Devices". The CD (Conference on Disarmament) established a committee in 1995 to begin work on an FMCT. The CD members in Geneva agreed by consensus to the so-called "Shannon Mandate[7]," which proposed for an "Ad Hoc Committee to negotiate a non-discriminatory, multilateral and internationally and effectively verifiable treaty banning the production of fissile material for nuclear weapons or other nuclear explosive devices"(CRS Report, Squassani, *etal.*2006). The CD was unable to reach a consensus on the mandate of the treaty as it did not specifically describe the scope of the negotiations (whether the scope of negotiations would apply only to future productions or would include existing fissile material stocks as well).

As this was the case, Ambassador Gerald Shannon "specifically" remarked that the mandate would include delegates' concerns on issues related to the scope of the treaty including existing stocks of fissile material, banning future productions, "or adding management of stocks" during discussions (Squassoni, *et al.* 2006:4).

FMCT at the Conference on Disarmament (CD)

Squassoni, *et al.*(2006) stated that after the conclusion of the Comprehensive Test Ban Treaty (CTBT) negotiations in 1996, "FMCT appeared to be the next priority." Nevertheless, there was no such consensus at the CD on a program of work. In late 1998, CD members agreed to establish an *Ad Hoc Committee* as a reaction to the Indian and Pakistani nuclear tests earlier that year. However, the CD was "unable to re-establish the Committee in 1999." They argued that four primary areas of work – "nuclear disarmament, prevention of an arms race in outer space (PAROS), negative security assurances, and a fissile material production cut-off"- were competing for priority within the CD. The 1998 session could not achieve any substantial progress because the contentious issues among CD member-states on the linkage between nuclear stockpiles and nuclear disarmament could not be resolved. Delegations from the non-aligned member-states wanted to put nuclear disarmament as the top priority agenda in the CD. Other delegates advocated keeping all agenda items in three broad categories, viz. nuclear disarmament, conventional disarmament, and other items (Moller and Sareva2014).

These four areas became important as several states preferred to link progress in one area to progress in another area. Quoting China as an example, Squassoni, *et al.*(2006) elaborated that China placed a condition for the start of FMCT negotiations. The condition was to start the PAROS negotiations, and other states followed suit. Hitchens and

Lauber (2010) wrote that the Ad hoc Committee did not reconvene as there wasno consensus on the CD's work program, which, by convention, is required by the Rule of Procedure. For the next ten years, the CD could not reach a consensus.

Including FMCT among a few outstanding unresolved issues in the CD made problems more acute in the CD. China's emphasis on linking FMCT negotiations with PAROS and nuclear disarmament hindered any possible progress in FMCT negotiations. Other member-states in the CD considered the issue of FMCT as the most important, thus preferring to keep it at the top of the priority list overany other issues. The United States National Missile Defense (NMD) program made Russia and China insist on negotiations on PAROS and nuclear disarmament, thus enabling the significant differences among the three powers to blockany progress in CD towardadopting a plan of action on FMCT negotiations. US-China conflicts on the approaches to FMCT and PAROS blocked any possible progress in the CD. The United States accused China of attempting to "block negotiations on FMCT by holding hostage to PAROS" (Moller and Sareva2014). Negotiations for an FMCT and other "substantive matters" on CD's agenda such as nuclear disarmament, PAROS,and negative security assurances (NSAs) – termed by CD delegatesas"coreissues"remained stalled till 2009.

A breakthrough came in May 2009 when the then outgoing President of CD, Algerian Ambassador Idriss Jazairy, tabled the draft decision, CD/1863, in CD for a program of work for the session. It drew no objections from the CD members and was adopted as CD/1864 the same year. The new program of work envisaged the establishment of four Working Groups instead of Ad Hoc Committees or co-ordinators. A close analysis of the four mandates revealed that the agreement on the establishment of the program of work was based on compromises by members did overtime on PAROS (by China), NSAs (by Non-Aligned Group), and, most importantly, the reversed stand of the United States on FMCT verification under President Obama administration. In his April 2009 speech in Prague, President Obama pledged that the United States would seek a new FMCT with averification mechanism that could end the production of nuclear weapons-usable fissile materials. The position under the Obama administration was in contrast to the US position previously held under President George W. Bush administration, which stood for an FMCT without verification provisions. The mandates of the Working Groups were:

- "to negotiate a treaty banning the production of fissile material…on the basis of (the Shannon Mandate)";
- "to exchange views and information on practical steps for (nuclear disarmament), including on approaches toward potential future work of multilateral character";
- "to discuss substantively, without limitation, all issues related to the prevention of an arms race in outer space"; and
- "to discuss substantively, without limitation, with a view to elaborating recommendations dealing with all aspects of (NSAs), not excluding those related to an internationally legally binding instrument" (Hitchens and Lauber 2010:8).

The word "cut-off" raised the question of whether an FMCT would cover only future[8] fissile material production or it would also include past productions by countries. The issue of whether the scope of the treaty negotiations would cover both existing and past production of fissile materials was the main focus during debates in the "Shannon discussions." It is still a matter of debate. The N-5(the United

States, UK, Russia, France, and China) and India believe that existing fissile stockpiles should be out of the purview of the FMCT negotiations. On the other side, countries such as Pakistan haveinsisted that if FMCT is to be effective, it has to consider the need for a broader scope including both existing stockpiles and future production of fissile material that could lead to "meaningful" nuclear disarmament. Given the "ambiguous nature of Israel's nuclear weapon status", countries such as Egypt and other Arab states insisted that all existing nuclear weapons-usable stockpiles should be put under international supervision and control, besides mandating to declare all weapon-usable fissile material stocks (Hitchens and Lauber 2010).

Another source of contention that hinders the progress in FMCT negotiations is the question of verification of fissile material stockpiles. An FMCT would indeed ban the production of weapons-usable fissile materials; the production of others would not be. Nevertheless, in order to ensure that the latter materials are not diverted for nuclear weapons programsor military uses, they should come under the surveillance of international inspectors, perhaps by the IAEA and it is possible if there is a strong provision for a verification mechanism in the treaty under negotiation (Persbo 2010).

Issues on the applicability of verification mechanisms, such as whether inspections would include both declared and undeclared sites, rights of countries, particularly NWS, to safeguard their national interests, rights of inspectors, are relevant issues in the negotiations' agenda. The scope of treaty negotiations requires fixing the goal of cut-off verification before coming into the question of what and how methods or measures are to be used to implement verification mechanisms under the treaty. The details of the verification mechanism is dealt with in greater detail in the next chapter while examining and analyzing the responses of the United States to external challenges to FMCT negotiations.

Significance of FMCT

There are many reasons for supporting FMCT. However, scholars and experts share different views on the importance of FMCT's significance. Based on the views, three different sets of views are analyzed one by one.

The **first** view is that FMCT would reinforce nuclear non-proliferation objectives. The basic logic of an FMCT has been that without fissile material in supply/stock to countries having aspirations to develop nuclear weapons, they would simply be unable to acquire nuclear bombs in the future. "The goal of the FMCT is to reinforce nuclear non-proliferation norms"(Burgess 2010: 13). He meant that the ultimate purpose was to achieve the goal of nuclear disarmament by preventing the production of plutonium andHEU.

Hitchens and Lauber (2010) wrote that banning fissile material production would reduce the materials available for the nuclear weapons production, which would, in turn, lower the risk of vertical and horizontal nuclear proliferation. They further argued that an FMCT would "aid the cause of nuclear disarmament by making reductions in nuclear disarmament irreversible."

Bunn (1998) observed that Russia, the US and the IAEA were engaged in trilateral discussions over safeguards on their excess weapons-usable stocks. These safeguards were meant tomake efforts to channel excess stocks to peaceful purposes irreversible.

Jonas (2006) argued that an FMCT is a "disarmament and non-proliferation tool" which would prevent further production of weapons-usable fissile material and enhance transparency and accountability for the excess stockpiles of fissile materials all over the world. He further argued that it "would prevent a future nuclear arms race and reinforce the commitments of the NWS and NNWS under the NPT."

Kimball (2013) stated that the non-nuclear weapons states that were parties to the NPT were already prohibited from producing or acquiring fissile materials for nuclear weapons. "An FMCT would provide new restrictions for the five recognized nuclear-weapon states(NWS)–the United States, Russia, the United Kingdom, France, and China)and for the four nations that are not NPT members (Israel, India, Pakistan, and NorthKorea)."

The second view on the significance of an FMCT is that it would significantly impact on the de-facto nuclear weapon states and non-nuclear-weapon states. Bunn (1998) observed that FMCT negotiations would provide an opportunity to engage India, Pakistan, and Israel (North Korea had not conducted a nuclear test then) apart from the N-5 to limit the weapons-usable fissile material. FMCTwould also, he argued, assuage the 1995 promise on the part of the N-5 to negotiate "such a treaty" in exchange for non-weapon NPT states' agreement to extend the NPT indefinitely.

Berkhout, Frans, Oleg Bukharin, Harold Feiveson, and Marvin Miller(1995) argued that for the N-4, except for China, "the chief purpose of a cut-off is to cap (and eventually rollback) the weapons programs of Israel, India and Pakistan." A universal cut-off, like the proposed FMCT, would make the above-mentioned three de-facto weapons states (India, Pakistan, and Israel) fall in the same line. They would be drawn into the nuclear non-proliferation regime by allowing their nuclear weapons programs for inspections and opening up the critical nuclear facilities to international inspectors. However, the authors also warned that inspections and supervision should not be restricted to existing weapons-usable materials but extended to the future production of unsafeguarded weapons-usable materials and "potential production facilities" also.

They argued that views of China on the cut-off issue were unclear as it had reservations about allowing the inspectors to its nuclear facilities and for its possible need for weapons- usable fissile materials. China might not want to get itself isolated from the N-4, so it was prepared to come along with the N-4 through an informal agreement. As for India, a "comprehensive" cut-off would be favorable considering India's long demand for a "non-discriminatory" FMCT.[9]

Chow Brian G., Richard H. Speier, and Gregory S. Jones (1995) stated that one objective of the then non-proliferation policy was to cap and eventually reverse the nuclear weapon programs in these (India, Israel, Pakistan, and North Korea) undeclared nuclear weapon states. Another objective was to prevent terrorists and other sub-national groups from gaining access to nuclear weapons or sensitive nuclear materials, i.e., plutonium or highly enriched uranium (HEU). Such materials were produced in the military and (some) civilian nuclear programs.

Jonas (2006) saw FMCT as a formidable step that would attract many states. He argued that if the four de-facto nuclear weapon-states (including North Korea) became FMCT parties; it would accelerate the involvement of many states in the FMCT,which would be a significant achievement. Jonas (2006) perceived FMCT negotiations as a platform for the United States to work hard to provide incentives to nations to avoid treading nuclear paths or relinquish them if they had already taken the path. While accepting that an FMCT would not solve all problems, he believed that halting fissile material production for weapons use would limit the opportunity of nuclear NWS for expanding the nuclear arsenals.

The third and final view on the significance of an FMCT is that it is "central to any effective international effort to minimize the accessibility of weapons-usable fissile materials to states, terrorist groups, and black marketers" (Berkhout, *et al.* 1995: 168). This argument is supplemented by Jonas (2006) when he observed that an FMCT would reduce nuclear proliferation risks, including the risk of nuclear terrorism. Verification of FMCT, it was argued, would promote a culture of "international responsibility" instead of "national concern", and this would lessen the risks of illegal diversion(Schapper2010:49).

However, Udgaonkar (1999) wasskeptical about the success of the proposed treaty without any substantial commitment from the "nuclear haves." He argued that inthe UNGA resolution (1993), which set in motion the negotiations of FMCT, the aim of nuclear disarmament was not mentioned. As far as Nuclear Weapons States (NWS) are concerned, they have not shown any commitment on their part of the bargain related to the NPT. The US relies on nuclear weapons to defend its security. From the American perspective, according to him, at a minimum, in order to enter into an FMCT, the United States must determine that its stocks were adequate to meet any future military requirement, especially for a treaty of potentially-unlimited duration.

US Position on FMCT: George W. Bush Administration

In July 2004, following a two-year review onthe fissilematerial treaty by the George W. Bush administration, the United States announced thatitcould support a legally bindingban on the production of fissile material intended for weapon use. However, this was reversed in 2006 by stating that the US could not support a legally binding FMCT under the "parameters of Shannon Mandate." In May 2006, the US delegate told CD members that it "sees no need at this time, however, for the negotiation of new multilateral agreements on nuclear disarmament, outer space, or negative security assurances." In May 2006, the United State stabled a draft treaty on FMCT alongwith a "White Paper" on FMCT. In June 2006, a US official told the CD that "..there is no - repeat, no - problem in outer space for armscontroltosolve"(Squassoni,*etal.*2006:4).

Significantly, the Bush administration's White Paper (2006) on FMCT to the CD contained no verification procedure (Burgess 2010: 25).

The White Paper (2006) on the FMCT made public by the US government states that the United States

> "...has given considerable thought to what an FMCT should look like. The draft treaty that we have put forward sets forth the essentials needed for an FMCT that would meet the objective of ending expeditiously the production of fissile material for use in nuclear weapons...Stocks of already existing fissile material would be unaffected by the FMCT. The production of fissile material for non-explosive purposes,such as fuel for naval propulsion, also would be unaffected by the treaty...
>
> The US draft treaty omits verification provisions, consistent with the US position that so-called "effective verification" of an FMCT cannot be achieved...The United States has concluded that, even with extensive verification mechanisms and provisions- so extensive that they could compromise the core national security interests of key signatories, and so costly that many countries would be hesitant to implement them-, we still would not have high confidence in our ability to monitor compliance with an FMCT" (the US Department of State,2006).

The White Paper cast doubts on an effective verification

mechanism. It argued that effective verification would require high compliance from member-states. Some states might resent to a proposal for an intrusive verification on the pretext that such verification could compromise their national interests. The White Paper further stated that the mechanisms and provisions for an effective verifications hould meet the reality – difficulties in the CD in negotiating for an international ban of fissile materials. These mechanisms and provisions, if not explicit, could make countries assume that these mechanisms and provisions would take care of possible violations, thereby relieving themselves relief from taking up individual or collective responsibilities toward making the world safe from nuclearproliferation.

President George W. Bush administration's proposal had no scope of verification provisions and hence an effective verification mechanism because of, perhaps, its judgment that an FMCT would not be verifiable. Jonas (2006) argued that verification of FMCT was "problematic", and hence the Bush administration refused to negotiate for a verification regime. The treaty, he continued, could not be signed unless the US convinced itself that its fissile stocks were enough for any future military requirement considering the treaty's potential unlimited duration if it entered into force. Hailing the administration's stand on an FMCT without verification provisions, he argued that the United States changed its position from the last stand of its "willingness and readiness" to negotiatean FMCT according to *Shannon Mandate* because it was not producing any concrete results. The United States' new position without verification was to allow negotiationsto proceed. The new position was seen as a forward step to allow FMCT to "finally gain tractions", which, otherwise, had been unable to progress for more than a decade. Reactions of Japan, Australia, and, quite interestingly, China were in the form of "muted disapproval" of the US position (Jonas 2006:604-605).

Burgess (2010) opined that the administration's proposal resulted from its "judgment that FMCT would not be in fact verifiable." The opposition to verification measures, he opined, might have also stemmed from the US Navy's resistance to allowing international inspectors to conduct oversight and monitoring of the US naval nuclear propulsion program.

However, Reif and Foley (2013) argued that theyrejected the US approach set forth by the George W. Bush administration in May 2006. They stated they supported the approach advocated by the privately organized International Panel on Fissile Materials (IPFM). The IPFM'sproposal, they argued, includes verification of an FMCT covering both future production and pre-existing stocks. These would be overseen by the IAEA Safeguards Division and "cover uranium facilities, reprocessing facilities, material declared in excess for military use, and HEU for use in naval propulsion reactor fuel." The IPFM suggested for expansion of the Safeguards Division to have an intrusive verification and to support it; a large budget would be made which would be contributed by the member countries.

In contrast to Jonas' (2006) argument that criticism of the George W. Bush administration's position on FMCT appeared to be politically motivated, Burgess (2010) argued that proponents of a verification regime maintain doubts about the verifiability of such a treaty are politically driven. Further, a verification system would also assure that permitted materials were less vulnerable to terrorist theft because they would be subjected to strict international supervision (Boese 2005). Nonetheless, the May 2006 US draft on FMCT had steered enough polarization on the issue of verifiability of a potential FMCT.

President Obama's FMCT Position: A Break from the Past

The May 2006 Bush administration's draft on FMCT,

ultimately, was overturned by President Barack Obama in April 2009 when he reiterated the US position in Prague (the capitalcity of the Czech Republic) that the US would seek a new FMC Treaty "that verifiably ends the production of fissile materials" intended for nuclear weapons and devices. In the speech, President Barack Obama announced changes intheUS nuclear weapons policy. The President stated:

> "...And to cut off the building blocks needed for a bomb, the United States will seek a new treaty that verifiably ends the production of fissile materials intended for use in state nuclear weapons. If we are serious about stopping the spread of these weapons, then we should put an end to the dedicated production of weapons-grade materials that create them. That's the first step."(The White House, 2009).

The Obama administration had chosen to pursue nuclear policies different from what his predecessor,President George W. Bush, had intended on FMCT. At least theoretically, the Obama administration's approach, seemed to be much closer to the CD/1864, which was adopted as the program of work by the CD in 2009. In a statement delivered by the then US Permanent Representative to the CD in March 2013, Ambassador Laura Kennedy reaffirmed the US position on FMCT. Shestated:

> "The US shares the international goal of a non-discriminatory treaty that halts the production of fissile material for use in nuclear weapons or other nuclear explosive devices, and that is internationally verifiable. An FMCT would be an important, international achievement, both for non-proliferationand disarmament. It would effectively cap the fissile materials available for use in nuclear weapons" (US Mission to the United Nations in Geneva 2013).

What prompted President Obama to take a call for a different approach to FMCT that seeks a verification mechanism to end the production of fissile materials intended to use for nuclear weapons is a big question that can be analyzed and debated. At the same time, it throws a significant challenge to many policy-makers and scholars alike to unlock. Nevertheless, it was then too early to have a final call on the US approach and intention on having an effective, multilateral, and non-discriminatory FMCT that serves as a stepping stone towards the goal of complete nucleardisarmament.

Analysis of the Two Different Positions

After its "extremely multilateral" beginning, President Clinton administration, by 1994, had fallen into the line of unilateralism under the influence of Congress which was dominated by Republicans[10]. In President Clinton's Nuclear Posture Review, "Counter-proliferation" was a part of the President's nuclear strategy. The nuclear first strike doctrine against "new enemies" ("rogue" states in particular) was very much in its military strategy. The multilateral orientation of the Clinton administration such as attempts to ratify the CTBT, secret efforts to bring more transparency to the nuclear complex, and others, began to fail by the secondhalfofthe1990s.TheRepublican-dominatedCongress, from 1996, blocked the CTBT, the Kyoto Protocol, the Bioweapons Convention, and a Convention to outlaw Anti-Personnel Mines. For example, in 1999, Republican Senator and the then Chairman of the Foreign Committee, Jesse Helms, managed to block CTBT ratification (Schaper and Muller 2004). Senator Jesse Helms opposed the CTBT and refused to table the treaty on the Committee's agenda. The Senator said, "...The effect of this treaty would be to forever forbid the United States from testing its nuclear arsenal while allowing the rogue nations of the world to proceed with their nuclear plans" (Ritchie 2009:48).

President George W. Bush entered the White House

with a team that was more "unilateral" and committed toward US military supremacy - more than any previous US government. The team included many prominent neo-conservative officials such as then Vice-President Dick Cheney, former Defense Secretary Donald Rumsfeld, former Deputy Defense Secretary Paul Wolfowitz, and a few others who had already pushed for a "forced regime change" in Iraq to contain Iraq's military in 1998. The security strategy of theBush administration was based on "absolute military superiority", where reliance on active nuclear weapons for deterrence and development of a more robust nuclear arsenal was incorporated - much like the Cold War era. For this, the Bush government was very reluctant to sign any binding disarmament treaties(Schaper and Muller 2004:18).

Indeed, the Bush administration's policies had no place for disarmament; instead, it focused on extending the life of nuclear weapons in its stock. So much emphasis on nuclear weapons was not given by earlier Presidents, except President Ronald Reagan during his first term when there was an unprecedented escalation of the Cold War. The Bush administration's Nuclear Posture Review, released in January 2002, and National Security Strategy (2002) report promised to use all kinds of means including the nuclear option to deal with emerging threats from "rogue nations" possessing WMD or terrorist groups. The administration's National Security Strategy of 2002 and 2006 articulated the doctrine of "pre-emptive"[11] actions against hostile states and terrorist groups seeking WMDs. The revolutionary change in the Bush administration's nuclear policy was making nuclear weapons a "usable necessary" means of war instead of a "weapon of last resort." It was argued that the United States should maintain reliable nuclear warheads that are active andresponsive and produce further cost-efficient additional warheads (Warren 2011).

In short, Schaper and Muller (2004) opined that

President George W. Bush administration's security policy had" almost no place for multilater alarms control and non-proliferation." Hence concerning verifying an FMCT, the position during the Bushadministration was exact – it should not go beyond the "absolute minimum necessary." The unilateralism aspect of the Bushadministration was relatively unambiguous as the administration failed to enter into various international agreements such as withdrawal from the ABM Treaty, withdrawal of its signature from the International Criminal Court, refusal to be part of the Kyoto Protocol, opposition to CTBT, maritime law, Biological Diversity Protocol, and Bioweapons Protocol. Hence, we can say that the administration's position on FMCT was consistent with the President's broad security policy and nuclear posture.

President Barack Obama came to the Oval Office with a new promise and enthusiasm to move toward changing the course of America's nuclear policy. President Obama took active steps since the early years of his first term to showcase his commitment to nuclear disarmament. In contrast to the Bush administration's hard effort for nuclear weapon reactivation and its prioritization in the US security policy and strategy, the Obama administration gave the same attention to non-proliferation and the country's weapons posture.

Under the Obama administration, the UnitedStates and Russia signed a legally binding replacement agreement to the Strategic Arms Reduction Treaty (START),which expired in 2009. The START was replaced by the New START that entered into force in February 2011. On September 24, 2009, President Obama chaired a UN Security Council Summit on nuclear disarmament andnon- proliferation – the first time a US President chaired a session of the UN Security Council. The Council unanimously adopted Resolution 1887, which called for accelerated efforts toward nuclear disarmament and laid down procedures to accomplish the goal. President Obama pledged to win Senate ratification of the CTBT. The White House had also reportedly initiated discussions with Pentagon about potential deep cuts to the US nuclear arsenals (Council on Foreign Relations 2013).

Holloway (2011) stated that President Obama set out his vision of a nuclear weapons-free world. To achieve this goal, the President, he wrote, was proposing that non-proliferation regime had to be strengthened through new institutions and mechanisms of enforcement so that a global nuclear order could be created whereby the violators would be severely punished to stop any repetition of such violation. The President argued that nuclear weapons states, in his words,"will get rid of their nuclear weapons only" if they were convinced that a non-proliferation regime could prevent states from breaking out and punish those that attempt to do so. Holloway (2011) opined that President Obama administration was clear about this connection between nuclear non-proliferation and nuclear disarmament.

In his National Security Strategy (2010), Warren (2011) wrote that President Obama accepted that the vision he set out, "the goal of a world without nuclear weapons," would not be fulfilled during his administration. Nevertheless, he believed multilateralism was the right approach to achieving a nuclear- free world. The Obama administration emphasized the need for cooperation with Russia and others to make states accountable for their obligations towards the goal. In the administration's Nuclear Posture Review (2010), the commitment to non-proliferation and the goal of elimination of nuclear weapons were included for the first time. This development was a complete shift from the Bush administration's nuclear posture.

However, President Obama made a "dual pledge." On the one hand, he talked of achieving the "goal of a world without nuclear weapons" and sidelining the Cold War thinkingby "reducing the role of nuclear weapons in national security strategy and urg(ing) others to do the same." On the other hand, he pledged to maintain a robust nuclear arsenal to deter any kind of threat by adversaries and guaranteed the same security to America's allies as well. In a nutshell, "the Administration has pursued a policy of nuclear balance" in which there are both components - steps for nuclear disarmament and measures to maintain US superiority and nuclear options (Warren2011:432-452).

Nevertheless, the President's Prague speech in April 2009 conveyed his vision for preventing nuclear proliferation, strengthening the international efforts for nuclear disarmament, and preventing nuclear terrorism (Warren 2011). Maintaining such vigor and enthusiasm for non-proliferation and nuclear disarmament seemed to have guided President Obama to accept an FMCT with a verification regime thereby reversing the previous US position on FMCT during President Bush administration. It was just the tip of the iceberg.

Role of Domestic Factors

The role of domestic factors in shaping the United States' position on FMCT and its implementation is significant. Just as international norms impact domestic discourse, domestic factors have their share in shaping the US position and influencing the US role internationally. The first sign of the international norm's impact is seen in domestic political discourse. Including many mechanisms and measures in the domestic laws through consensus in Congress and executive supportwould enhance the salience of international laws and procedures. As a leading actor, the USin the international efforts to contain nuclear proliferation and nuclear disarmament, should first address the significant domestic hurdles to project itself as an unflinching supporter of "the goal of a world without nuclear weapons." This is because changes in the domestic discourse would precede and accompany changes in the international discourse towards the goal (Cortell and Davis 2000: 66-69).

President Clinton entered the White House in 1993. Having a Democratic President and a Democratic-controlled Congress, many people from the strategic community, particularly from the disarmament community, expected a change of direction in the country's nuclear policy "towards a minimum deterrent posture" (Ritchie 2009:55). The President, in September 1993, proposed for an FMCT to stop production of weapons-usable fissile material. It was accepted warmly as an important step within the United States. During the Clinton administration, there was a push to shift in the direction of unilateralism in arms control and non-proliferation efforts from the administration's modest beginning with multilateralism. The push was unsurprisingly from the Republicans who had stormed the Congress after the 1994 US midterm elections. The election results brought more Republicans to the House and the Senate of Congress (Schaper and Muller2004).

Ritchie (2009) pointed out that the 1994 Nuclear Posture Review, which examined the purpose and nature of the US nuclear forces after the Cold war, was a half-hearted attempt to reduce nuclear weapons by the United States as it simultaneously envisaged a strategy to respond to any Russian revival or reform by retaining America's supremacy in nuclear forces. The review retained America's focus on strategic triad and time-bound nuclear rearmament on a large scale. Many Congressmen and influential voices outside the government questioned the government's stand to acquire such large nuclear forces or arsenal at its disposal. However, Senator Strom Thurman argued that Clinton administration had de-emphasized the role of nuclear weapons too far and criticized its plan for nuclear cuts.

Ritchie (2009) stated that there were concerns over the lack of attention given to nuclear forces by senior-level political and military officials during the Clinton administration. It appeared tomany within the strategic community that Clinton administration was drifting toward a direction without long-term impact[12] and with resources insufficient to maintain a robust, modern, and survivable counter-force nuclear arsenal accompanied by "renewed commitment" to revitalize the nuclear weapons production complex. Such views came to dominate nuclear weapons policy under Bush administration.

The Bush administration continued the policies on the nuclear arsenal and production complexwith much vigor – a Cold War legacy. Weapons modernization and development of new kinds of weapons under the 2005-06 *Reliable Replacement Warhead (RRW) and Complex 2030 plan*[13] were also sanctioned by The administration's Nuclear Posture Review (2001) and the National Security Strategy (2002 and 2006), respectively. The lack of senior-level serious political and military attention on nuclear weapons led to a drift towards a sense of neglect in nuclear weapons policy. This was "exacerbated by the absence of bipartisan consensus" in Congress on the "long-term future of nuclear weapons policy." The reasons such as the end of the Cold War; and other issues of national security importance such as Russia, China, and non-proliferation concerns explained why there was little attention from thesenior-level officials. These issues came on top of the priority list for the Pentagon and the White House. These reasons explain the evolution of nuclear weapons policy under the Bush administration (Ritchie 2009:58-59).

For the Bush administration, it was not challenging to reject the verification regime in FMCT negotiations. The Republican-controlled Congress under President Clinton (after the 1994 US midterm elections) and President George W. Bushhad resisted attempts to constrain US strategic deterrence capabilities such as the deployment of missile Defense systems, US capability to test nuclear weapons, developing a new type of nuclear weapons, etc. President Clinton's decision to sign the CTBT sparked serious debates in Congress and outside. The Senate responded to President Clinton's effort by voting against the CTBT in 1999. President George W. Bush did not want to repeat it. In both Presidencies, there was strong resistance to the nuclear disarmament goal despite President Clinton administration's frequent suggestions that it was moving towards the goal (Ritchie 2009:61-66).

The President showed his optimism and commitment to nuclear non-proliferation and disarmament agenda in his famous April 2009 Prague speech. The goals he declared in the speech were reaffirmed in his administration's National Security Strategy (2010), the Nuclear Posture Review, and the New START Treaty. Nevertheless, it was not the same when President Obama set his feet in the White House. There was bipartisan support when he pledged that the United States would enter into an effectively verifiable FMCT negotiation in2009.Thus, the Democratic Party-dominated Congress during the first two years of the Obama administration yielded to the President's pledge.

Reifand Foley (2013), stated that within the United States, bipartisan support existed for a verifiable FMCT. Thebipartisan Congressional Commission on the *Strategic Posture of the United States*, and as the *Council on Foreign Relations Task Force on US Nuclear Weapons Policy*, endorsed a verifiable treaty that would end the production of fissile material for weapons purposes. On June 3, 2009, Senate floor statement, Senator McCain endorsed an FMCT by emphasizing the role of IAEA to use the tools to ensure a world free of nuclear weapons.

However, Reif and Foley (2013) argued that strong

Republican opposition to President Obama's nuclear disarmament proposal persisted. Former Senator John Kyl (R-AZ) and Senator Jeff Sessions (R-AL) led "the charge against the Comprehensive Test Ban Treaty (CTBT). So, it remains to be seen if enough Republicans would support a verifiable FMCT to ensure ratification."

The United States and the United Kingdom usesHEU in nuclear submarines. The HEU can be diverted for weapons use, if necessary, by them. The United States has a reserve of 100 tons of HEU for this purpose. There are advantages of using HEU instead of LEU in military submarines. It makes less noise and can be used for years without refueling. The other reason is that using HEU makes the reactors in submarines comparatively smaller than using LEU (Schaper 2010).

There have been strong calls from the international community that the FMCT should cover the HEU used in naval propulsion. There are several reasons for this. First, the HEU and submarines are kept secret, which means there is no knowledge whether it is being diverted for military purposes. Secondly, the conversion of HEU to LEU is a progressive step toward non-proliferation and nuclear disarmament, and it is a feasible transition. Third, the vast reserve of HEU could last for decades (Schaper 2010). It is an advantage for any country, including the United States, to look for a developing new variant of submarines that LEU fuels. Moreover, finally, if nuclear disarmament is to be achieved, it is to be strived for. For this, there is no need for further production of HEU and hence no need to exclude naval propulsion fueled by HEU (Schaper and Muller 2010: 57-58).

A letter circulated in the CD for reference of the member-states by the then Permanent Representatives of Canada, Japan, and the Netherlands in September 2009 envisaged that theuse of HEU in naval reactor fuel was against the "integrity" of FMCT. It strongly discouraged the use of HEU in naval propulsion and put its fear of diversion for nuclear weapons.

It recommended that states make every effort to minimize the use of HEU for both the military and civilian purposes.

Ma and Hippel (2001) argued that should the United States convert HEU to LEU as reactor fuel, as France did, "it could meet the proposed requirements of the FMCT as delineated by those who advocate extending the FMCT to the production of fissile material for naval propulsion." Ma and von Hippel regarded converting from HEU to LEU as reactor fuel desirable; however, the United States Navy did not view it as such (Burgess2010:14).

Burgess (2010) argued that the suggested conversion to LEU has certain vital disadvantages for the US Navy,and the US Navy has strong reservations about the mandate of the proposed FMCT that would include nuclear propulsion in strategic submarines as well as the involvement of the IAEA. He argued, for example, according to a report to the US Congress in 1995, the Director of the Office of Nuclear Propulsion (ONNP) stated that replacing by LEU would reduce the core life for Trident-class submarines and Nimitz-class aircraft carriers equipped with 45-year cores, to 14 and 10.4 years respectively. In this light, Burgess argued that the US Navy had adopted a prudent and cautious approach keeping in military reserve all the fissile material usable for naval propulsion.

Significantly, the US poses one of the major hurdles for realizing an effective, verifiable, and non-discriminatory FMCT.

Notes

1. According to Squassoni, *et al.* (2006), enrichment plant technologies "include gaseous diffusion, electromagnetic isotope separation, laser isotope separation, and gas centrifuge isotope separation(which Iranis developing)."

2. Spent fuel contains uranium and radioactive fission products. Reprocessing is the process of separating Pu-239 from the spent fuel of uranium. Plutonium in spent fuel cannot produce the required nuclear yield, and it is required to be separated from spent fuel, and this production is referred to as "reprocessing."

3. The term international community is quite uncertain; the exactness of its meaning can be contested, although it is widely used. The term is misleading because nothing is consensual regarding an international issue that affects almost all the member countries of the UN or the world. Consensus and unanimity are very rare yet the 'international community' is widely used as if any decision by some countries (mostly powerful and big states) is presented as a legitimate one agreed upon by all without any objections and reservations. Having said this, since it is a widely accepted term, the tradition of its usage is followed.

4. According to United Nations Office at Geneva(UNOG)2019 data, the member-states at the CD count 65 in numbers. See, *http://www.unog.ch/80256EE600585943/(httpPages)/6286395D9F8DABA380256EF70073A846?* Open Document

5. Two events preceded the 1993 address by President Clinton to the United Nations. In 1989, the former Soviet Union announced a cessation of HEU (high-enriched uranium) production and the planned shutdown of all plutonium production facilities by 2000. They further proposed negotiating a multilateral agreement for a verified cut-off based on IAEA safeguards. In 1992 President George H. W. Bush announced that the US would no longer produce plutonium or HEUf or nuclear weapons.

6. In December 1993, the UNGA passed Resolution 48/75L entitled, "Prohibition of Production of Fissile Material for Nuclear Weapons or Other Nuclear Explosive Devices."

7. In its 1994 session, the CD appointed Canadian Ambassador Gerald Shannon as a Special Coordinator. Over the next year, Ambassador Shannon consulted with CD members, and in March 1995, the CD adopted the"Shannon Report"

4

US Responses to External Challenges to FMCT Negotiations

Different views and opinions on the scope and feasibility of an FMCT from the participating members-states during FMCT negotiations have been a characteristic feature of the Conference on Disarmament (CD). Some countries and national experts agree to the view of an FMCT covering both past and existing stockpiles of fissile material if FMCT is to address nuclear disarmament effectively, while others have been opposing this position since the beginning of negotiations. The issue of an effective verification mechanism in FMCT negotiations has been a barrier to the quick progress of the negotiations in the CD. The US position on FMCT verification is clear and has been elaborated on the previous chapter. There are specific primary challenges from some foreign countries (external challenges) to FMCT negotiations. The chapter has attempted to answer the following three fundamental questions.

- What are the external challenges the US faces?
- What are the US responses to external challenges to FMCT negotiations?

- How the US responds to the challenges?

The disagreement in CD, mainly on the scope of the FMCT, is a stumbling block to the progress of FMCT negotiations. The US responses, though ambivalent, would push FMCT negotiations to a higher level of progress. The chapter is divided into two interrelated sections: *first,* the chapter examines and analyzes the external challenges to the FMCT negotiations; *second,* it analyzes the US responses to these external challenges. The first section attempts to bring out the contentious issues which have resulted in an impasse in the CD.

CD Member-States and FMCT Negotiations

It is imperative to know how CD delegates are divided on FMCT negotiations to understand the various issues that constitute a significant barrier to the quick progress of FMCT negotiations. The United Nations Office at Geneva (2019) stated that there were 65 (sixty-five)formal member-states in the CD. In the CD, there are groupings. The CD groupings are divided based on specific interests and objectives. These groupings often comprise like-minded member-states working in tandem as caucuses to serve their objectives and interests. According to Reaching Critical Will (2014), a disarmament program run by peace and freedom-loving women in Europe and North America, the CD groupings include the Western Group (mainly comprised of western advanced industrialized nations such as the United States, the United Kingdom, Canada, France, Germany, Australia, Spain, and a few Asian developed or semi-developed nations such as Japan, the Republic of Korea, Turkey, etc.); the Group of 21 (commonly known as "G21", and include countries mainly from the third world such as India, Pakistan, Myanmar, Venezuela, DPR Korea, Brazil, Islamic Republic of Iran, Syria, Senegal, Morocco, and others); the Group of East European states (Russia, Ukraine, Belarus, Kazakhstan, Romania,and Bulgaria); P-5 (five permanent members of the UN Security Council/ the five nuclear weapons states), and the P-4 (P-5 excluding China) and China (often refers to as Group of One). The agendas of these groupings and their approaches to the issues in the CD are discussed in this chapter. Decisions in the CD are made by consensus among the member-states.

CD delegates often disagree on some contentious issues or others. The trajectory of the FMCT negotiations in the CD has been more of dilly-dallying than progressing towards effective and efficient FMCT negotiations. Many times, FMCT negotiations were marked by its inability to establish a Working Group/Committee to bring negotiations back on the table, which reflects the limitation of working through consensus rule. A delegate or a few national delegates guided by their so-called "national interests" blocked many CD's initiatives, which ruined chances of bringing a consensus in the CD.

For example, a draft proposal (CD/1624) by the then Ambassador of Brazil, Celso Amorim, in the August 2000 session in the CD was on similar lines to a previous proposal by then Belgian Ambassador, Jean Lint. The Brazilian proposal contained four separate Ad hoc Committees to deal with fissile material, Prevention of Arms Race in Outer Space (PAROS)[1], nuclear disarmament,and negative security assurances. However, this proposal could not convince China. China held that the proposal did not see the issues of fissile material and PAROS on equal terms. It viewed that while there was a proposal for FMCT negotiations, only the discussion mandate was proposed for PAROS. Thus, the session could not resolve the conflicts, so the prospect of bringing a consensus in the next session remained a dream. The *Amorim proposal* got many supporters. Canada, New Zealand, South Africa, and others saw in the proposal a realistic mechanism to protect the interests of those who did not want to see the CD transformed into a mere talking hub based on some "thematic discussions" without substantive ground-work (Moller and Sareva 2014).

The CD delegates resumed FMCT negotiations in May 2009 according to the 1995 *"Shannon Mandate"* after a long lost decade since 1998 due to a lack of consensus at the CD. The CD adopted CD/1864 as its program of work. However, a few hurdles remained to be crossed by the CD, such as consensus on choosing the chairs of Working Groups and special coordinators (CD/1867) and a draft calendar of activities (CD/1866) from the then President of the CD, Argentine Ambassador R.G. Moritan. China and Pakistan were not ready for the drafts (CD/1866 and CD/1867), although the Western Group and Eastern European Group expressed their support for both drafts.

In the following years, attempts to strike a consensus in the CD on FMCT negotiations went futile due to opposition by countries from G21, particularly Pakistan, thereby prompting the then Japanese Ambassador to call for a consideration replacing the "consensus rule" in the CD. Pakistan refused to engage in FMCT negotiations which did not address the inclusion of pre-existing fissile material stockpiles. There were even suggestions from delegates from Canada, Ireland, Mexico, and a few others to start informal meetings among the delegates to sort out outstanding issues outside the CD if it failed to produce a negotiating forum, before proper negotiations on FMCT could start. It was struck down by delegates from Algeria, the United Kingdom, Pakistan, and Brazil. During CD's 2010 session, Pakistan's Ambassador, ZamirAkram, clarified that delegates could utilize the option of FMCT negotiations outside the CD that Pakistan would not oppose. However, Pakistan would not participate in such negotiations. Till the 2014 session's first part (held from 20 January to 28 March), the CD had not come out with a program of work on FMCT negotiations and other related issues. Delegations could not reach a consensus on the scope and details of an FMCT (Moller and Sareva 2014).

External Challenges to FMCT Negotiations

External challenges to FMCT negotiations are diverse. Since the CD delegates are comprised of member-states having different backgrounds and statuses in the international system, the challenges are complex and different from one member- state to another member-state. As mentioned on the above page, each grouping in the CD represents a loose confederation of different member-states cutting across their national boundaries. They act as cohesive groups and effectively make an impact at the CD where there exists every possibility of great power domination. The challenges are mainly concentrated on the scope and details of an FMCT. Former German Ambassador Bernard Brasach, in his farewell statement at the CD, in July 2009, observed that there was a relationship between scope and verification, and they had to be treated in parallel. He said that "they have to be fine-tuned neatly to each other in parallel throughout the negotiations" (Caughley 2009).

The scope of an FMCT ranges from provisions to include pre-existing and future fissile material stockpiles to verification mechanismsunder an international body, particularly the IAEA. Caughley (2009) opined that the treaty coverage (to use his words, "the actual extent of the production ban") would affect FMCT negotiations on what range of verification mechanisms could be needed to ensure compliance with the provisions from member-states. It means that treaty coverage of pre-existing fissile material stocks, for example, would require member-states to negotiate on what range of verification mechanisms would be implemented to ensure full treaty compliance from member-states. One crucial issue has been the diverse opinions among delegates on the exactdefinitionoffissilematerials,thatis,whattoinclude in the fissile material category. Some member-states in the

CD insist on including fissile material declared in "excess," such as weapons-usable material which is declared no more required for nuclear weapons development, during negotiations apart from pre-existing and future fissile material stockpiles (Hitchens and Lauber 2010:11).

Within the verification issue, there are various interrelated issues. These issues can be broadly classified into three. First, there are numerous debates among CDdelegates on whether to include intrusive verification in naval propulsion of member-states using HEU as submarine fuel; whether verification would cover undeclared nuclear facilities. The second issue is on debates as to which safeguarding authority would ensure compliance as per verification provisions. The debates have revolved around whether the IAEA-based NPT safeguard system would be applied to the proposed treaty with the IAEA as the sole authority or whether there would be alternative verification mechanisms and approaches. The third issue is related to debates on the costs of verification. An intrusive verification mechanism, if the negotiators agree on it, could cost millions of dollars. The issue of sharing the costs would be a delicate one consuming both time and political will.

Scope of FMCT Negotiations

The section attempts to highlight the external challenges posed by different groupings and countries in the CD in a holistic manner. An analysis of FMCT by the Nuclear Threat Initiative (NTI) (2013) revealed two primary issues in the FMCT negotiations: verification and pre-existing stocks. Concerning the issue of pre-existing stocks, under the 2009 International Panel on Fissile Materials' (IPFM) FMCT draft, verifying an FMCT covered both future production and pre-existing stocks (Reifand Foley 2013). The 1995 *Shannon Mandate* specifically did not preclude these states from raising this issue in negotiations.

Sethi (1998) statedthat the US, Canada, the United Kingdom, and France (a few member-states of the Western Group) viewed the *Shannon Mandate* as being confined only to the future production of fissile material for weapons besides insisting on a delinking of the issue with that of disarmament. The United Kingdom and France also insisted that the treaty must not limit their production of plutonium and HEU produced for civilian use. The P-5 states emphasize that "the most efficient route to nuclear reductions is through negotiations among themselves" (Hippel 1999: 36). Hippel (1999) stated that, among the NWS, the three (the UK, France, and China) insisted that the United States and Russia had to take the lead. In March 2013, the CD discussed an FMCT. Representatives from the United States, Canada, Australia, Japan, and the European Union argued in favor of an FMCT that firstly banned the productions of fissile material for nuclear weapons and other explosive devices (NTI2013).

Australia submitted a working paper to the CD in September 2010. The paper stated that the FMCT negotiating mandate banning fissile material production "implicitly means further production." Thus, it argued that a way to push the negotiations ahead would require accepting the FMCT negotiating mandate as dealing only with a future production of fissile material. However, the paper also stressed the need to develop a mechanism to make states declare all pre-existing fissile material stocks and place excess stocks of fissile material under verification measures voluntarily (Conference on Disarmament 2010).

By contrast, several Western-developed countries have pressed firmly for including pre-existing stockpiles of fissile material in an FMCT so that there would be semblance and sharing of burden between the nuclear-weapon states (NWS) and non-nuclear-weapon states (NNWS) (Dunn 1999: 9). Hippel (1999) stated that the "Group of 21" (G21) and other countries would like the P-5 to commit seriously to nuclear disarmament by including their pre-existing stocks of weapons-usable fissile material in the FMCT negotiating mandate.

A letter circulated by Permanent Representatives from Canada, Japan, and the Netherlands in the CD (September 2009) for the reference of the member-states envisaged for undertakings by the member-states. It stated that member-states would not divert pre-existing fissile material stockpiles, including civilian stocks, HEU used for naval propulsion, and excess fissile material stocks declared "excess to weapons and other military purpose." The letter implicitly discussed including pre-existing fissile material stockpiles of nuclear-capable states in FMCT negotiations. It also recommended establishing a system under the IAEA which could monitor fissile material stock for future use in naval propulsion facilities or other military reactors as fuel and materials from weapons declared excess for military use. The letter took note of the United States' large HEU reserves,which the US declared excess for weapons use but has reserved for future use as fuel for naval-propulsion reactors. It said that, although HEU has been reserved for military purposes, the US must not use it innuclear weapons or other nuclear explosive devices (Conference on Disarmament 2009).

Hitchens and Lauber (2010) argue that the importance attached to managing excess weapon-grade fissile materials is enormous given that the NPT's obligations on the NWS and the "moral and political pressures" on those that are not a party to the NPT, including the de-facto nuclear weapon states. Article VI of the NPT has great significance. It accompanies commitment from nuclear-capable states to reduce nuclear arms and to declare that fissile materials from the decommissioned nuclear weapons would be placed under an international safeguard system. This would diminish the globally available fissile material stocks irreversibly and transparently.

The case for the inclusion of pre-existing fissile material in the FMCT negotiations' mandate was highlighted in a joint working paper dated 9 June 2011 submitted to the CD by Bulgaria, Germany, Mexico, the Netherlands, Romania, Spain, Sweden, and Turkey. It argued that although the *Shannon Mandate* provided an excellent platform for FMCT negotiations on whether to include or exclude pre-existing stockpiles, the paper stated that FMCT negotiations should include these stocks since the pre-existing fissile material stocks posed a "proliferation risk" (Conference on Disarmament 2011). During the 2013 first session of the CD, delegations from Iran, South Africa, Switzerland, and Ireland argued that an FMCT addressing pre-existing fissile material stockpiles would address nuclear non-proliferation effectively. Previously, in May 2012, Iran, Syria, and Switzerland had argued for the inclusion of pre-existing fissile material stockpiles in FMCT negotiations (NTI 2013). Feiveson (2010) wrote that the inclusion of pre-existing fissile material stocks would neither make IAEA monitoring more difficult nor would it result in inaccessibility by international inspectors to weapons facilities.

In a letter dated 15 August 2003 from the Permanent Representative of Japan addressed to the CD's Secretary-General (CD/1714), Japan suggested FMCT negotiations in the CD based on future production cut-off without linking to the issue of pre-existing stocks to overcome the impasse in the CD (Conference on Disarmament 2003).

A letter dated 25 June 2012 from the Permanent Representatives of Germany and the Netherlands addressed to the CD's Secretary-General (CD/1935) mentioned the assertion by Tim Caughley, Residential Senior Fellow at UNIDIR. He stated that political issues concerning the pre-existing stocks could be resolved in experts' meetings over technical issues. In the letter, Tim Caughley opined that instead of dealing pre-existing stocks within the FMCT negotiations directly, it "would be subjected to a phased multi-faceted approach", wherein binding commitments from the nuclear weapons states were declared unilaterally or multilaterally (Conference on Disarmament 2012).

South Africa submitted a working paper entitled "The Possible Scope and Requirements of the Fissile Material Treaty (FMT)." The paper (CD/1671) stated that the issue of inclusion of past production of fissile material stocks had political and practical problems. However, it stated that fissile material already declared as excess could be included as a "baseline" at entry into force of FMCT. The purpose of the working paper was "to ensure irreversibility" of the material declared excess by putting such materials under verification measures. This could be a solution to the problem of the controversial issue of pre-existing stocks in the CD (Conference on Disarmament 2002).

Five former presidents of the CD (Ambassador Mohamed Dembri of Algeria, Ambassador Rodolfo Reyes of Columbia, Ambassador Juan Enrique Vega of Chile, Ambassador Jean Lint of Belgium, and Ambassador Henrik Salander of Sweden) took the initiative in the third part of the 2002 CD's annual session on a program of work and distributed among the CD-delegates. The proposal by the five former Ambassadors, known as the*"A5 Proposal"*, called for pre-existing fissile material stocks "to be included in the scope of the future FMCT negotiations", which was different from the 1995 *Shannon Mandate,* widely regarded as the basis for the future FMCT negotiations (Mollerand Sareva2014).

The *"A5 Proposal"* could not be adopted at the CD because of lingering disagreements between member-states, particularly between China and the United States. China held that FMCT progress should be linked to progress in

Prevention of Arms Race in Outer Space (PAROS) which the US rejected. China and Russia[2], despite the stalemate in the CD, have brought up the issue of PAROS several times. China had placed a draft on re-establishing an Ad Hoc Committee on PAROS and its mandate (CD/1576) in 1999, urging the CD to start negotiations for a treaty on PAROS. Similarly, a letter dated 5 June 2001 from the Permanent Representative of China (CD/1645) proposed for a treaty titled "Treaty on the Prevention of Weaponization of Outer Space" (Conference on Disarmament 2001). China, especially, linked its support for an FMCT to the United States' acceptance of a treaty on PAROS. It also fears that FMCT might limit its capacity to produce more nuclear arsenals to balance relatively more massive nuclear arsenals possessed bytheUnitedStatesandRussia,respectively(Reif2009).

In June 2002, at the 907th plenary session of the CD, China, Russia, and five other nations (Vietnam, Indonesia, Belarus, Zimbabwe, and Syria) submitted a "joint working paper" proposing a treaty (CD/1679) on PAROS. The paper's fundamental element was to secure an obligation not to use weapons in outer space (NTI 2013). A summary of PAROS by Reaching Critical Will (2014) outlined that in February 2008, both China and Russia submitted a "draft treaty for a ban on weapons in outer space" (CD/1839). It was titled "Treaty on the Prevention of the Placement of Weapons in Outer Space, the Threat or Use of Force against Outer Space Objects" (PPWT) on the CD, which contained many elements outlined in the 2002 working paper. On 10 June 2014, Russia introduced an "updated draft" to the CD in which there were many new changes; most importantly, the definition of "outerspace" was removed.

However, it was referred to often in CD deliberations. The 2003 annual session, *"A5 Proposal"*, continued to garner support from most member-states including China. In August 2003, China and Russia changed their previous positions that FMCT negotiations should go hand in hand with work on the treaty for PAROS. On 7 August, China, Russia, and Ukraine stated that they had accepted the PAROS mandate as Belgian Ambassador Jean Lint suggested on 26 June. On behalf of Five Ambassadors (A5),Ambassador Jean Lint, suggested amendment to the text they had proposed on PAROS.

Among the de-facto nuclear-capable states, Israel's case is unique. Although Israel has not blocked international efforts to conclude an FMCT, its policy rejects joining an FMCT[3]. Datan (2010) suggested that Israel did not believe that FMCT would serve its cause. Israel brought up two concerns in the statement to the UNGA First Committee in 2014.

Israel firmly holds the view that an FMCT would not have a significant effect on the Iranian nuclear program (Datan2010).First, it says that nuclear disarmament issues should be linked to achieving long-term peace and reconciliation in the West Asian region. This could be possible when regional security threats are resolved, and stability in the region is achieved. Secondly, Israel believes that FMCT does not address the challenges posed by non-compliance withinternational obligations by states and more pressing challenges posed by "misuse and un-checked dissemination of nuclear fuel cycle capabilities" among countries.

Thus, Israel seems to have serious apprehension of an FMCT that would compel Israel to accept verification measures that could jeopardize its activities required to maintain a weapons program. Having said this, Israel conducts its disarmament diplomacy quite tactfully. Though it has not ratified the CTBT, it has been actively participated in international efforts against nuclear non-proliferation and disarmament. Israel's engagement" in the design of its on site verification arrangements", for example, highlights Israel's attempt to project itself as a responsible nuclear state that supports international efforts "on nuclear safety, security and non-proliferation" (Datan 2010:36-45).

Nayyarand Mian (2010) opined that Pakistan maintained its position explicitly of including pre-existing fissile material stockpiles in FMCT negotiations. Pakistan argues that global pre-existing fissile materials could be diverted to build nuclear weapons. However, it has refrained, like many nuclear-capable states, from making public its exact size of fissile stockpiles. Pakistan has been arguing for declaring fissile material stocks and an FMCT that would include the pre-existing stocks. Pakistan argues that progressive reduction in fissile material stockpiles by member-states would effectively enhance the cause of nuclear disarmament. Pakistan seems to rely on India's position not to include past fissile material productions as India has the edge over Pakistan on the amounts of fissile material stockpiles. Pakistan's concerns about India's comparatively more considerable accumulation of fissile stockpiles can be gauged from the following statement by its representative in the CD.

On 18 February 2010, Pakistan Ambassador Zamir Akram explained tothe CD member-states that Pakistan's opposition to FMCT wasstrongly connected with India's position on FMCT. He stated that the FMCT negotiating mandate based on the *Shannon Mandate* would not address existing stockpiles which, he claimed, put Pakistan in an "unfavourable position vis-a-vis India", and it also singled out Pakistan (Moller and Sareva 2014). A report by UNIDIR (2013) explained Pakistan's unpreparedness for many CD initiatives from the start of FMCT negotiations. It explains that Pakistan wants to proceed when it is convinced that FMCT would be a non-proliferation measure, and an FMCT would also strengthen nuclear disarmament initiatives.

Nayyar and Mian (2010) wrote, "Pakistan may be willing to accept any declarations and monitoring arrangements concerning fissile materials and warheads as long as India also accepts them. Pakistan may be reluctant, however, to provide access, at least in the near term, to scientists and managers in its nuclear weapons program."

The 2009 session adopted a program of work (CD/1864) by the CD, which subsequently established a working group with the task of negotiating an FMCT based on the Shannon Mandate. However, Pakistan's consistent opposition to it made the CD unable to implement its program of work. In 2009, after the CD adopted CD/1864, Pakistan argued thatit would not accept FMCT negotiations without the mandate addressing the pre-existing fissile material stocks as it would not be able to implement the treaty. In March 2010, Pakistan, along with a few member-states of G21, argued that the draft proposal on a program of work tabled by the then CD President, Ambassador Abdul Hannan (Bangladesh), needed to amend for improvement and it would be done after taking all the views from the G-21 member-states. In February 2013, Ambassador ZamirAkram of Pakistan delivered a statement at the CD re-iterating Pakistan's refusal "to engage in direct, indirect or even pre-negotiations on an FMCT that did not address stockpiles." Pakistan and Egypt blocked initiatives in the 2013 annual session and hence could not establish a program of work (NTI2013).

Pakistan had also raised issues such as conventional arms control at regional and sub-regional levels and issues related to missile control at the CD, linking it to CD's first agenda - nuclear disarmament and cessation of arms race agenda. In August 2011, Ambassador ZamirAkram delivered a statement on behalf of the G21 reiterating the G21's commitment tonuclear disarmament. Ambassador Akram also brought in the need to have a legally binding agreement on negative security assurances (NSA) (Nayyar and Mian 2010). Significantly, Pakistan remains an important barrier to the smooth progress of the FMCT negotiations at the CD.

Issues on FMCT Verification

The issue of verification of an FMCT is technically complex, politically controversial, and economically costly. Acton (2010) stated that verification of nuclear disarmament accompanied a high level of technical challenge as there could not be a surety that nuclear-capable states would not possess significant fissile material stockpiles for military uses. To prevent such uncertainties, he suggested, there should be some mandatory steps taken by these states themselves, such as collection and disseminating information about fissile material production and placing those inputs in the public domain.

The use of HEU as submarine fuel in naval propulsion reactors has many benefits, such as low noise, expanding submarine's working duration, and least refueling. Despite these benefits, scholars, and experts maintain that HEU should either be replaced by LEU or FMCT negotiations should include international verification on naval propulsion reactors for several reasons.

First, the HEU and submarines are kept secret, which means there is no knowledge of whether it is being diverted for military purposes. Secondly, conversion of HEU to LEU is a progressive step towards non-proliferation and nuclear disarmament, and it is a feasible transition. Third, the massive reserve of HEU can last for decades (Schaper 2010). Feiveson (2010) has argued that naval fuel cycles have to be kept under IAEA monitoring to ensure that it has not been diverted to nuclear weapons purposes. The final treaty should require a state to declare to the IAEA how much HEU it would require for fabricating new naval-reactor cores.

There have been strong calls from the international community that the FMCT should cover the HEU used in naval propulsion. A letter circulated in the CD for reference of the member-states by the then Permanent Representatives of Canada, Japan, and the Netherlands in September 2009 envisaged that the use of HEU in naval reactor-fuel was against the "integrity" of FMCT. It strongly discouraged the use of HEU in naval propulsion and put its fear of diversion for nuclear weapons. It recommended that statesmake every effort to minimize the use of HEU for both militaryandcivilian purposes (Conference on Disarmament 2009).

Burgess (2010) argued that building a regime that would have the necessary financial support, andtechnical capability to verify a country's capacity to·produce fissile material was a distant project. Moreover, he argued that the pledges given by the US that no fuel ever put under the international safeguards be withdrawn for military purposes didnot apply to the US Navy. The strict and intrusive verification measures outlined under the proposed FMCT would hurt the US national interest as the US, like Russia, has strict reservations about revealing the core policy on fuel cycle and naval reactors scanned by external agencies. Moreover, other P-5 member states would not accept the FMCT (intrusive) verification for naval propulsion.

Besides, there are issues such as whether IAEA should be the sole authority (agency) entrusted with the verification of an FMCT, whether to include an undeclared production facility and who should bear the cost of FMCT verification that is on the table of FMCT negotiators. Pellaud (2010) wrote that the response on the question of who should be entrusted with the verification of an FMCT would be a political issue and, hence, political consensus among member-states would be required. An article contributed by the IAEA (2010) suggested that FMCT verificationmeasures "would benefit by paralleling the existing IAEA safeguards systems."

Hitchens and Lauber (2010) wrote that if FMCT

negotiators chose the IAEA and agreedto use existing verification measures, FMCT could be provided with the current "IAEA-based NPT safeguard system." The safeguard system for the NNWS (non-nuclear weapons states) was designed as such to conclude on the peaceful use of all declared nuclear material in a state and the existence of undeclared nuclear material or activities in a state. The IAEA's 1997 Additional Model Protocol helps the agency to conclude the existence of undeclared nuclear material or activities effectively. Thus, for NNWS, whichh as IAEA's comprehensive safeguard agreements and has acceded top Additional Protocol, would not have to take extra additional burden if the negotiators choose the NPT safeguard systems.

US Responses to External Challenges

External challenges to FMCT negotiations are varied and complex to resolve. Responses from the United States have been amorphous. The chapter has examined and analyzed the responses from the United States.

On the issue of the scope of FMCT negotiations, that is,inclusionorexclusionofpre-existingfissilematerialstocks of nuclear-capable states, the United States' position has been unambiguous. The US White Paper (2006) on FMCT stated that the United States

> "would meet the objective of ending expeditiously the production of fissile material for use in nuclear weapons. The basic obligation under such a treaty, effective at entry in to force, would be a ban the production of fissile material for use in nuclear weapons or other nuclear explosive devices. Stocks of already existing fissile material would be unaffected by the FMCT. The production of fissile material for non-explosive purposes, such as fuel for naval propulsion, also would be unaffected by the treaty."

On 31 May 2012, the CD held a "thematic discussion"

on FMCT. The US delegate reiterated Washington's position that an FMCT "should only cover new production of fissile materials" (NTI 2013). In March 2013, during discussions in the CD on FMCT, the United States, alongside Canada, Australia, Japan, and the European Union, argued that FMCT negotiations should ban future production of fissile material for nuclear weapons first (NTI 2013). It is reported on the NTI site that in November 2013, the United States started consulting "with key nuclear powers along with India and Pakistan" on revitalizing FMCT negotiations.

Ambassador Laura Kennedy of the United States, in a statement she delivered in May 2013 in the CD, said that "For the US, CD 1864 is still the one Program of Work that commanded consensus and remains for us the touchstone for a balanced and comprehensive approach" (US Mission to the United Nations in Geneva 2013). The CD adopted CD/1864 (2009) through consensus as to its program of work. CD/1864 envisaged establishing four separate Working Groups, including one to negotiate an FMCT based on the 1995 *Shannon Mandate.* In a statement in March 2013 to the CD, Ambassador Kennedy stated that attempts by some member-states in the CD "to address existing stocks multilaterally and link them to a ban on a new production for weapons purposes will only complicate consensus on beginning a negotiation on an FMCT" (US Mission to the United Nations in Geneva 2013). Thus, the US responses to "the extent of production ban," that is, whether to include/exclude pre-existing fissile material stocks in theFCMT negotiating mandate, have been consistent and clear.

On a question raised by Press in January 2011 on what the US was doing to address Pakistan's concerns about asymmetry viz-a-viz India if FMCT negotiating mandate covers only future production ban of fissile material, former US Bureau of Arms Control, Verification and Compliance, Assistant Secretary Rose Gottemoeller responded that the

US believed every country had the right to raise its concerns and CD would discuss the issue and take a consensus. However, she stated that the US was holding dialogue with Pakistani delegates at the CD and did express her hope that Pakistan would understand the importance of the CD/1864, which was an outcome of consensus rule in the CD, in pushing forward FMCT negotiations (US Mission to the United Nations in Geneva 2011). Ford (2007) wrote that the US has also been "unilaterally reducing its own stockpile of fissile material." It has been cooperating with Russia to eliminate surplus fissile materials from the weapons stocks of each country, thereby committing itself to ensure that no such fissile material for nuclear weapons use exists anywhere.

Since the mid-1990s, the US and Russia have declared almost one and a half tons of fissile materials in excess in their weapons stocks. Of this, one and a half Highly Enriched Uranium (HEU) has been down-blended[4] to LEU. Even after the conversion, about 20 percent of the HEU global stocks remained to be down-blended to LEU or used as HEU. The disposition of "weapons-grade plutonium" that both the countries declared excess for weapons use did not begin (Meerburg and Hippel 2009).

Institute for Science and International Security (ISIS) (2013) estimation puts the amount of US declaration as 226 ton of fissile material (174 tons of HEU and 52 tons of plutonium). ISIS (2013) states that the US approaches the question of the disposition of HEU declared excess has both unilateral and multilateral dimensions. The US disposes by placing fissile material declared as excess under IAEA safeguards, and it did place 12 tons of fissile material under voluntary IAEA safeguards through the end of 1998. The United States has been down-blending excess HEU to LEU even though a large amount of HEU in fuel reactors remains to be down-blended to LEU.

Ma and Hippel (2001) argued that the United States could comply with their proposed version of an FMCT by banning the production of fissile materials for weapons and extending it to any weapons-usable fissile materials for any military use, including naval propulsion reactors. They further argued that if the FMCT were to be upheld by allparties, countries joining in the nuclear navy propulsion "club" would have to switch their fuel supply to Low Enriched Uranium (LEU). They, citing the French example, say that the US could shift from HEU to LEU.

To maintain a balance between the need to put these fissile materials declared as excess under international safeguards and the need to protect sensitive nuclear information vital to the host's national interests, such as fuel reactor designs from nuclear inspectors, the US, Russia, and the IAEA launched a "Trilateral Initiative" which involved the need to develop different verification approaches to be applied at specific facilities in the US and Russia, where declared excess fissile materials were stored. The United States adopted a "dual-track" plutonium disposition policy in the late 1990s. It does, together with the N-4 and some states, make annual, voluntary declarationsto the IAEA in the form of INFCIRC/549(the IAEA's Guidelines for the Management of Plutonium) declarations. The United States has already a version of Model Additional Protocol "identical" to the one established by the IAEA in 1997. However, the United States' version has an exceptional clause that allows the US government to exclude any activity that could lead to access by the IAEA that could harm US national interests significantly (Meerburg and Hippel 2009).

However, the United States' responses on issues such as PAROS and FMCT verification mechanism highlights incoherence. Hence they are amorphous. The United States rejected a draft proposal by China (CD/1576) in 1999 urging for re-establishing an Ad Hoc Committee on PAROS to negotiate a treaty (legal instrument) on PAROS. The United States in a letter dated 26 June 2002 (CD/1680), declared that it opposed negotiation of a treaty on outer space arms control. The US argued that the existing agreements such as the Limited Test Ban Treaty (1963) and Outer Space Treaty (1967), formally named the Treaty on the Principles Governing the Activities of States in the Exploration and Use of Outer Space, including the Moon and Other Celestial Bodies, were sufficient for promoting"peaceful uses of space" and re-affirmed its commitment to both the mentioned treaties (Conference on Disarmament 2002).

The February 2008 Russia-China joint draft treaty (CD/1839) on PAROS submitted in the CD was rejected by the George W. Bush administration characterizing the initiative as "a diplomatic ploy by the two nations to gain a military advantage" (Reaching Critical Will 2014). A letter dated 19 August 2008 (CD/1847) from the Permanent Representative of the United States in the CD explained the US objections to such a proposal. It argued that the US policy consistently opposed any moves to constrain its right to accessspace-based information and activities. The letterstated that the US had the right to "conduct research, development, testing, and operations in space for military, intelligence, civil, or commercial purposes" (Conference on Disarmament 2008). Hence, the US did not see any reason as to why it would support a treaty on the prevention of arms race in outer space arms in the CD (Conference on Disarmament 2008). The 2006 US National Space Policy reiterated the US preservation of US right to develop capabilities in space and took actions to protect its space activities.

On 28 June 2010, the Obama administration announced its new "National Space Policy of the United States of America." The policy, however, marked a shift in both language and tone compared to the 2006 US National Space Policy. The Bush administration's policy was comparatively

US-centric. Foust (2010) wrote that "the Bush policy spoke only of interference with US space systems, while the Obama policy refers to interference with any nation's space systems."

The Obama administration, however, continued to oppose the 2008 China-Russia draft treaty. In a statement delivered by then US Permanent Representative to the CD, Ambassador Laura Kennedy, on 8 February 2011, it was explained that the 2008 PPWT, outlined in the CD/1847, as proposed by China and Russia did not meet the criteria of equitability and effective verifiability as outlined under the 2010 new US National Space Policy. She stated:

> "For one, the text does not contain prohibitions on the testing or deployment of terrestrially-based anti-satellite weapons of the kind China tested in January 2007, generating almost 3,000 (2750) pieces of space debris. It is also not effectively verifiable, which both Russia and China acknowledged in CD/1872. The draft PPWT does not include an integral, legally binding verification regime for effectively monitoring compliance with its obligations" (US Mission to the United Nations in Geneva 2011).

She stated the US believed that the PPWT is "fundamentally flawed and provides no basis for a negotiating mandate in the CD for a binding arms control agreement" (US Mission to the United Nations in Geneva 2011). The United States, she said, would continue to support inclusion of a "non-negotiating, or discussion, mandate, in any consensus CD program of work" underthe agenda item known as PAROS (US Mission to the United Nations in Geneva 2011). However, former Assistant Secretary of State for Bureau of Arms Control, Verification and Compliance, Ambassador Rose Gottemoeller, stated inher statement to the CD in January 2012 that the US did not see the possibility of the CD negotiating on the four "core issues" (FMCT, nuclear disarmament, negative security assurances, and

PAROS) simultaneously. The Ambassador expressed the US position that the CD should focus on FMCT negotiations first (US Mission to the United Nations in Geneva 2012).

On the verification issue, the United States had blocked many important initiatives by member-states of the CD. George W. Bush administration did not consider a verification mechanism with strong provisions in an FMCT necessary to progress. The Bush administration was adamant about any move that attempted to undermine US efforts to maintain a robust and dynamic national security strategy where a few small and active nuclear weapons played an important role indeterrence (Schaper and Muller 2004).

Even if FMCT went through the process of verification ratification, it would not be easy to achieve. In July 2004, US Ambassador Jackie Sanders announced that the United States did not hold that an FMCT would be verifiable. Subsequently, it blocked a consensus of a resolution sponsored by Canada which had been adopted in 2003. The Resolution titl'ed "General and Complete Disarmament: Taking Forward Multilateral Nuclear Disarmament Negotiations" urged the CD to commence negotiations on a "non-discriminatory, multilateral and internationally and effectively verifiable treaty banning the production of fissile material for nuclear weapons or other nuclear explosive devices"(NTI2013).

Jonas (2006) highlighted the American concern of foreign spies in the guise of nuclear inspectors that could risk the country's nuclear security. This is because safeguards and inspections are done multilaterally under the banner of an international specialized organization. He further arguedthat given the difficulty of resolving any one of the issues, deletion of a verification regime which is one of the most contentious matters in an FMCT could pave the way for successful FMCT negotiations rather than impede progress.

In 2005 meetings of the UNGA First Committee, Brazil, Canada, Kenya, Mexico, Sweden, and New Zealand governments proposed a draft resolution to establish Ad Hoc Committees on four issues including that of an FMCT as envisaged in the *"A5 Proposal."* The United States blocked this initiative. In May 2006, the United States tabled its draft treaty and a "White Paper" on FMCT. The White Paper mentioned that "...The US draft treaty omits verification provisions, consistent with the US position that so-called 'effective verification' of an FMCT cannot be achieved..."(USA White Paper 2006).

There came a drastic shift from this position of an FMCT with no verification provisions to one with a verification mechanism after President Obama came to power. In his Prague speech in April 2009, he proposed a verifiable FMCT and reiterated the Obama administration's commitment to an effective FMCT with a verification mechanism (The White House 2009). In the final plenary meeting of the CD held in March 2010, the United States Permanent Representative to the CD, Ambassador Laura Kennedy, delivered a statement to the CD stating that the 2010 US Nuclear Posture Review would help in reducing the number and role ofnuclear weapons in the US national strategy. She also pointed out the United States' interest in discussing "core issues" in the CD and its commitment to launching FMCT negotiations (US Mission to the United Nations in Geneva 2013).

In her statement in March 2013 to the CD, Ambassador Laura Kennedy reiterated the US stand that it shares the"international goal of a non-discriminatory treaty that halts the production of fissile material for use in nuclear weapons or other nuclear explosive devices, and that is internationally verifiable" (US Mission to the United Nations in Geneva 2013). The Ambassador also said that verification obligations should cover "only the new production of fissile material." She said that the US would take voluntary measures and other necessary agreements with other countries such as the ongoing US-Russia Plutonium Management and Disposition Agreement (PMDA), to address verification of pre-existing stockpiles. The PMDA, for example, commits both sides to dispose of at least 34 metric tons of excess weapons-grade plutonium under the supervision of the IAEA (US Mission to the United Nations in Geneva 2013).

On the issue related to verification of US naval propulsion reactors using HEU as fuel, Washington continues to have reservations about an intrusive verification of its naval reactors. Burgess(2010) argued that the suggested conversion to LEU had certain essential disadvantages for the US Navy and the US Navy had strong reservations about the mandate of the proposed FMCT that would include nuclear propulsion in strategic submarines as well as the involvement of the IAEA. There is no direct official statement or declarationon this aspect from Washington.

Meerburg and Hippel (2009) wrote that facilities, including those where nuclear fuel was fabricated for naval propulsion reactors, could conceal fissile material production activities. The Department of Defense, they wrote, demanded the US government to use the US Additional Protocol with the IAEA to exempt reporting to the IAEA of all its sites. A statement by the former Acting Under Secretary for Arms Control and International Security to the CD, Rose Gottemoeller, in February 2014 reflected Washington's general stand on FMCT verification. Gottemoeller stated that the US and the UK hadstarted consultations on developing "verification procedures and technologies", which have been shared with other P-5 nations. The US and its P-5 partner, according to her, would consult closely on various contentious issues related to definitions and other important aspects such as modalities to be applied for a verifiable and multilateral FMCT (US Mission to the United Nations 2014).

Notes

1. Prevention of Arms Race in Outer Space (PAROS) is a UN resolution that re-affirms the fundamental principles of the 1967 Outer Space Treaty and advocates for a ban on the weaponizationof space. The PAROS resolution acknowledges the limitations of existing laws related to outer space and recognizes that the Outer Space Treaty "by itself does not guarantee the prevention of an arms race in outer space" (Federation of American Scientists 2014). The resolution advocates for further measures to prevent an arms race in outer space by, among other things, urging all state parties, particularly those with space capabilities, to adhere to the objectives of PAROS. Besides, it calls on the Conference on Disarmament (CD) to establish an ad-hoc committee regarding PAROS resolution issues. See *http:// fas.org/programs/ ssp/nukes/ArmsControl_NEW/nonproliferation/ NFZ/NP-NFZ-PAROS.html.*

2. Russia officially support a verifiable FMCT that bans future productions of fissile material for nuclear weaponspurposes.

3. Prime Minister Benjamin Netanyahu, after establishing an Ad-hoc Committee at the CD to begin FMCT negotiations in 1998, stated that"We will never sign the [Fissile Material Cutoff] treaty, and do not deludeyourselves- no pressure will help. We will not sign the treaty because we will not commit suicide." SeeAluf Benn, "The Struggle to Keep Nuclear Capabilities Secret," Ha'aretz, 14 September1999, URL:*http://fissilematerials.org/library/gfmr08cv.pdf.*

4. The process through which HEU (having more than 20% concentration of U-235 or U-233) is converted to LEU (generally having 12% to 19.75% concentration of U-235) is termas the down-blending of HEU. Fresh LEU isused in research reactors.

5

Initiatives Under the Trump Administration and India's Stand

FMCT Negotiation Status under Trump Administration

The FMCT is a promising treaty that is expected to be different from the Non-Proliferation Treaty (NPT). From the American perspective, nuclear proliferation presents a grave danger to its security and the international community. While an FMCT will not solve all problems, capping the amount of fissile material available for nuclear weapons use will be a good step toward combating the proliferation of Weapons of Mass Destruction (WMD). The US would want to prevent nuclear terrorism. A multilateral FMCT would not even require any usingof counter-proliferation measures or pre-emptive strikes.

The US appears to be committed to a legally binding treaty to maintain the statusquo since it had already stopped producing the two fissile materials,viz. plutonium, and HEU alongwith Russia, United Kingdom, and France. The Obama administration seemed prepared to accept verification provisions in the proposed FMCT, but skepticism remained, and it remains. Today, there is no clarity as to whether it would allow a strict and intrusive verification as proposed by many scholars and some countries. The US does maintain some reservations, such as access to naval fuel reactors in naval propulsion. This is a paradox. The claim for an effective FMCT has to go through a set of strict and intrusive verification mechanisms, yet transparent and non-discriminatory measures appear unlikely.

In April 2015, a Group of Governmental Experts (GGE)[1] issued a report. The report recommended that the FMCT negotiations to take forward for a future treaty. It also identified areas of convergence and divergence in critical aspects for further negotiations. During the NPT Review Conference 2015, the United Kingdom, on behalf of the P-5 members, issued a joint statement stating their "support and readiness"[2] to negotiate the FMCT. In March 2016, the United States formulated a proposal[3] on the FMCT. It was well-received on the CD by many member-states. Irish representative praised the American initiative. The draft to establish a working group to negotiate an FMCT was circulated by the then Nigerian president at the 65-member CD. The new proposal by the US calls for the establishment of a working group so that an internationally agreeable and effectively verifiable treaty dealing with the fissile materials for "use in nuclear weapons or other explosive devices."

The Trump administration mentioned that it would support the negotiation of an FMCT at the 2018 NPT Preparatory Committee. In July 2018, the United Nations a High-level FMCT Expert Preparatory Group report, advocating that "negotiations for the FMCT should continue, despite the lack of significant improvements in negotiations" (NTI 2018).

With this background, a summary of the status of FMCT negotiations under President Donald J. Trump administration could be laid out. Under the administration, the US continued to support and reaffirmed its commitment to have an effective FMCT negotiation provided that crucialmembers such as Pakistan and China, in particular, cooperate. The US committed to the international proposal of a strict moratorium on producing fissile material used in nuclear weapons and other explosive devices along with the United Kingdom, France,and Russia. The US believed that "such a step is an example of the type of 'effective measure' – within the meaning of Article VI of the NPT – that would help create an environment that is conducive to future nuclear disarmament" (the US to the CD,2019).

The US believed that the CD's failure to have a concrete launching action for an effective and consensus-driven FMCT was not inherent. Instead, it believed that it was the result of a continued lack of will from a few member-states who were yet to commit for an agreement on the proposed ban on the production of fissile materials. In other words, these "key states"were not prepared to cap their stocks of fissilematerials for nuclear weapons. Thus, the US push for effective, verifiable FMCT negotiations under the Trump administration revolved around two conditions:

a. that the negotiations in the CD were inclusive of all 'key states' and were based on mutual consensus.

b. that the United Statesremained opposed to any attempt to include existing stockpiles of fissile material in an FMCT–a continuation of the position for mulated under the Obama administration.

Thus, the US saw the Conference on Disarmament (CD) as a platform that fulfilled these conditions, and it remained a leader in the CD for an FMCT that effectively curbed the global proliferation of nuclear weapons and to see that global disarmament measures were effectively implemented. The US strongly backed FMCT as a nuclear non-proliferation measure that would reduce fissile material stockpiles sans an intrusive verification mechanism involving its naval reactors.

India and FMCT Negotiations

Among the de-facto nuclear-capable states, India is against expanding the scope of production ban covering pre-existing/past productions. Israel's unique case has been discussed in the previous chapter.

Although India supports the position of some key Western developed countries about excluding pre-existing stockpiles of fissile material from the cut-off agreement, it differs with them on the issue of linkage of the FMCT with nuclear disarmament. India and Pakistan, the two prominent member-states of G21, have been insisting to link "fissban" to the broader objective of nuclear disarmament in CD's negotiations for an FMCT (Sethi 1998).

Udgaonkar (1999) echoed this point and argued that if the proposed FMCT was to be effective, it had to be enmeshed to the overall goal of a nuclear-weapons-free world (NWFW), which was the goal of the Canberra Commission. The Commission laid down the specificity and steps to reach the goal of nuclear disarmament without compromising on states' security. He stated that the non-commitment nature towards nuclear disarmament of NWS was a sign of their lack of transparency and hampered the efforts toward achieving irreversibility in the disarmament process.

Tellis(2001) wrote that Indian strategic interests coincide with a "progressive drive" in the direction of complete disarmament. India and the United States hardly have had any conflict on the need to halt nuclear proliferation. He wrote that even as India did not sign the NPT and the CTBT India remained committed to signing anon-discriminatory, multilateral and effective FMCT assuming it to be a treaty that would support the nuclear non-proliferation regime. Nevertheless, it is unlikely to sign an agreement that would requiring India to open up to the complete verification of existing stockpiles. This is because he explained that a hegemonic power like the United States would influence the policy-making of any foreign country concerning its nuclear decision-making. This also applied to any freedom of choice in nuclear decision-making that "India nationally enjoys" (Tellis 2001).

Mian, Zia, M.V. Ramana, and R. Rajaraman (2010)stated that India's conditions on nuclear disarmament efforts were based on the principles of multilateralism and non-discrimination. A fundamental criterion for India's refusal, the authors identified, to FMCT negotiations covering pre-existing fissile material stocks would be the nuclear forces of China (in particular), France,and the United Kingdom. China's arsenal and fissile stocks matter greatlyto theIndian nuclear policy-making community. India's stockpile of fissile material (weapons-grade plutonium) is much less than China's HEU and weapon-grade plutonium reserves.

Thus, India does not want to commit to an FMCT that would halt India's options to achieving parity with China. India wants to avoid joining such treaties that would require revealing details about the status of its pre-existing stockpiles of fissile materials or "past production histories." Moreover, India does not want to give up the production of HEU, which is used as fuel for its nuclear submarine. It is unwilling to shift to LEU as fuel as itmight hamper progress in the further development of the nuclear submarine.

India's Stand and Prospects

Arms control and FMCT proponents know that many aspects of an FMCT have been too controversial. In the context of multilateral negotiations at the Conference on Disarmament (CD), it means that consensus-building to ink the final deal on issues such as verification regime, the scope of the treaty, and permissible activities under the treaty have been hard to attain. There are uncertainties regarding what the proposed treaty might look like. The only certainty could be if there is to be one, multiple decisions that would have to be made regarding the obligations of signatory states (Jonas 2006). Each of these decisions would have a major impact on the overall non-proliferation regime and the extent to which the nature of the FMCT would be.

In the ongoing geopolitical churning, an assertive China becomes a hurdle in India's deserved quest for integration into the global nuclear order. One such example of China's interference is the blocking of India's entry into the Nuclear Suppliers Group (NSG). In this context, India's current stand concerning FMCT negotiations remains justified for two reasons.

First, it gives India considerable autonomy in exercising its capability to re-orient its nuclear posture if required. The fact that India shares its land boundaries on two sides with Pakistan and China leaves India with no option but to make its nuclear policy flexible.

Second, the US has a balanced nuclear weapons policy. Evaluation of the Trump administration's nuclear weapon policies indicates that while the US desires a verifiable FMCT that effectively bans the production of fissile material, it has taken a firm nuclear security policy. The Administration has not formally outlined its stance on nuclear disarmament and modernization. In 2018, President Trump announced his plan to withdraw from the 1987 Intermediate-Range Nuclear Forces (INF). In August 2019, the US completed withdrawal formalities, leaving the future 2010 New Strategic Arms Reduction Treaty (New START) in limbo. It was, perhaps, done in response to Russia's missile build-up around Europe despite the treaty. Furthermore, this was in response to China's (not a party to the INF or the START) increasing military and conventional missile build-up in the Pacific.

In short, it would be fair to state that the nuclear weapon policies of the Trump administration closely follow that of the Obama administration. The mere difference is that theUS2010 Nuclear Posture Review (NPR) under President Obama emphasized reducing nuclear stockpiles and delivery mechanisms worldwide. Whereas the same under President Trump administration (2018 NPR) focused on renewed efforts to deter and effectively match Russia and China while showing interest in extending the New START.

India's future course of action is closely linked to the roles played by the US and other key states in the CD. Pakistan's insistence on including the existing stockpiles as a pre-condition for negotiations will remain a defeated voice. India should build a resilient partnership with the US and allies to push for an effective and verifiable FMCT despite the opposition. This could be done without compromising India's core principle – maintaining its sovereign right in decision-making. This resolution will test India's negotiating capabilities on a major global platform. A considerable amount of diplomatic energy needs to be invested in convincing China in this direction. The Shannon Mandate should remain the foundation for India's stance on FMCT negotiations.

Notes

1. It was established by the United Nations General Assembly (UNGA) to push forward the FMCT negotiations in theCD.
2. Source: *https://www.nti.org/learn/treaties-and-regimes/proposed-fissile-material-cut-off-treaty/*
3. Source: *https://www.armscontrol.org/act/2016-03/news/us-floats-new-fissile-talks-formula*

Conclusion

Negotiations for Fissile Material Cut-offTreaty (FMCT) represent a strong effort on the part of the international community to reinforce nuclear disarmament goals. An FMCT is a much-needed treaty that would supplement arm reduction treaties such as the New START Treaty between the United States and Russia, which will remain in force till February 2026. The United States has been cautious about nuclear weapons and their use since the end of the Second World War. National security policies of the United States have been formulated keeping in view strategic competitions in its vicinity and parts of the world. The US security policies during the Cold War had a vital element of nuclear weapons use as a deterrence strategy against any potential attacks by adversaries. Nuclear weapons policy was a core element in its national security and foreign policy formulations during the entire Cold War period.

The United States' approach to non-proliferation initiatives has been ambiguous. The US approach lacks consistency and concreteness. Pressing security challenges determine its policy approaches. Even the Clinton administration's attempt to reduce nuclear weapons was half-hearted as it simultaneously envisaged a strategy to respond to any Russian revival as a potential global rival by retaining America's supremacy in nuclear forces. At times nuclear non-proliferation initiatives of the US take the rear seat when pressing national security challenges such as bolstering strategic and economic relationships with allies and friends comeup.Lack of consistency in the US approach gave rise to failures in preventing nuclear detonation by countries such as India and Pakistan in 1998 and by North Korea in 2006.

Attempts to stem nuclear proliferation have often depended on who occupies the White House. Hence, we could see nuclear policy shift from the president to the president, including that from President George W. Bush administration to President Obama administration. The Bush administration focused more on strengthening the US nuclear arsenal than on weakening others or preventing the proliferation of nuclear weapons. The Bush administration Nuclear Posture Review (NPR) of 2001 put the threat of the use of nuclear force as a core element of US national security policy. The NPR of 2001 and the National Strategy on Weapons of Mass Destruction of 2002 supported the idea of the use of nuclear weapons against a non-nuclear weapon state. The Bush administration's nuclear weapons planning guidance explicitly stated that the United States might use nuclear weapons against any adversary (ies) in response to their chemical or biological weapons use against it or its allies.

President Bush administration unilaterally abrogated the Anti-Ballistic Missile (ABM) Treaty; refused to work for ratification of the Comprehensive Test Ban Treaty (CTBT) by the US Senate, and even rejected the idea of a verifiable Fissile Material Cut-off Treaty (FMCT). All these steps ran counter to non-proliferation initiatives by his predecessors. However, there came a shift in Washington's approach to nuclear proliferation and nuclear disarmament after President

Barack Obama came to power.

The Obama administration's vision of "a world without nuclear weapons" was in starkly contrasted with the Bush administration's nuclear policy. Obama's assertion in support of a nuclear-free world encompasses strengthening of NPT, ratification of the CTBT, and efforts to push for a verifiable FMCT in the CD besides working to make nuclear weapons safe from terrorist hands. In September 2009, President Obama chaired a UN Security Council Summit on nuclear disarmament and nuclear non-proliferation. The Council unanimously adopted Resolution 1887, which called for accelerated attempts to promote nuclear disarmament efforts, laying down some desired actions to accomplish the goal.

President Obama believed in multilateralism, and his administration's Nuclear Posture Review of 2010 called for cooperation with Russia and other countries to make states accountable for their obligations towards the goal of "a world without nuclear weapons." President Obama's proposal of an FMCT with a verification mechanism did open a window of opportunity for renewed negotiations in the Geneva-based Conference on Disarmament. The Obama administration chose a prudent approach to FMCT making a U-turn from the previous Bush administration's nuclear posture. It supported the establishment of a verification mechanism in line with the CD/1864of2009.

While the Obama administration set out a vision of a world free from nuclear weapons, it was yet clear whether it would be able to cope with the external and domestic challenges against its vision. The debate on the desirability and feasibility of a world free from nuclear weapons did generate many supporters and opponents within the United States. Even though eminent US personalities, namelySam Nunn (former Senator), Henry Kissinger (former Secretary of State), George Schultz (President Reagan's Secretary of

State), and William J. Perry (former Secretary of Defense) has supported the idea of a nuclear-free world. The differences over the feasibility of such an idea within the US Congress are sharp. Even though Republican Senators such as Senator McCain and others did endorse an FMCT, there is hardly unanimity of views.

The question is, however, not confined only to the realm of internal political differences. There has been a large gap between the country's leadership professed and what is practiced. For instance, a report by the Congressional Budget Office in 2013 signaled an investment of billions of US dollars ($335 billion) for development and modernization of new generations of modern weapons in the next ten years. The report also suggested President Obama's call for more investment in restoring national laboratories and modernization of storage facilities that maintain US nuclear weapons stockpiles. This proposed modernization of nuclear weapons, coupled with the US Congress' refusal to ratify the CTBT, gave an impression to the outside world that all that the US President proclaimed were reflective of his nuclear policy rhetoric. That the rhetoric aimed to make other countries fall in line without any genuine commitment toward nuclear disarmament.

Despite the changed US position on FMCT, the CD continues to be in a stalemate without any concrete program of work to push FMCT negotiations. On deeper introspection, it is found that CD delegates have not come to a consensus to kick-start serious discussions and deliberations to sort out all the contentious issues on scope, verification, costs, and other major issues hurdles to FMCT negotiations. The Group of 21 or G21, comprising of Non-Alignment member-states, has been sticking to the goal of nuclear disarmament and pressuring the CD to put the disarmament agenda onthe top priority list among the CD agendas. While a prominent G 21 member-state such as India maintains that FMCT should focus on the ban of future fissile material stockpiles, other prominent G21 member-states such as Pakistan and Egypt have been demanding that FMCT negotiating mandate include pre-existing fissile material stockpiles as well to enhance the nuclear disarmament agenda effectively. Indeed, Pakistan has been a significant hurdle to the FMCT negotiations in the CD since the beginning. Pakistan's argument in the CD reflects its reliance on India's position. It, most of the time,opposes what India proposes.

India,and a few leading member-states of the Western Group, in the CD, viz. the US, the United Kingdom, Canada, and France view that FMCT's negotiating mandate confine only to the future production of fissile material for weapons. While India has a similar stand, there is a stark difference. India has linked FMCT negotiations to the issue of complete disarmament. On the other hand, the US and some of its allies base their position on FMCT ontheir professed goal of promoting nuclear non-proliferation.

Countries such as Germany, Spain, Turkey, Iran, Switzerland, Mexico, Bulgaria, the Netherlands, Sweden, and a few others have expressed their view to include pre-existing fissile material stockpiles in the FMCT negotiations since these stocks pose a nuclear proliferation risk. The *A5* proposal in the 2002 CD annual session made a strong case for the inclusion of pre-existing fissile material stocks in the scope of the future FMCT negotiations, which was different from the 1995 *Shannon Mandate*-widely regarded as the basis for the future FMCT negotiations.

The *A5 proposal* could not be adopted in the CD properly due to lingering disagreements among CD member-states. China and Russia have proposed linking PAROS with FMCT. They have blocked many CD proceedings which did not address their concerns adequately; with support of Vietnam, Indonesia, Belarus, Syria, and a few others. The

United States, on the other hand, has rejected the Russia-China joint draft treaty of 2008 on PAROS, arguing that it challenges the US freedom to explore space, harness its potential peacefully and safeguard its national security interests.

Also, a country such as Israel, a close strategically of the US, has a distinct approach to FMCT. Israel seems to have serious apprehension of an FMCT that would compel Israel to acceptverification measures.It does not believe that FMCT would further strengthen nuclear disarmament goals.

Regarding FMCT verification, the US has proposed a conditional verification mechanism. It wants to exclude its naval propulsion reactors that use HEU (highly enriched uranium), a fissile material, from the verification regime. Whereas France has blended down HEU to LEU to use as naval fuel in propulsion reactors, the US continues to rely on HEU as fuel even though efforts to blend-down excess fissile materials, particularly HEU, had been taken up in the past.

There are arguments from experts about the pledges given by the US that no fuel ever put under the international safeguards would be withdrawn for military purposes do not apply to the US Navy. The US Navy has the unique option to withdraw HEU under international safeguards for use in naval reactors. However, it does not do so because such an attempt would create political uproar and would undermine US efforts to stem nuclear proliferation as well. The strict and intrusive verification measures outlined under the proposed FMCT would hurt the US national interest as the US, like Russia, has strict reservations about revealing the core policy on fuel cycle and naval reactors scanned byan external verification authority. The US Navy has strong reservations about the mandate of the proposed FMCT that would include nuclear propulsion in strategic submarines as well as the involvement of the IAEA. The US has expressed its willingness to take voluntary measures and other necessary agreements with other countries to address the verification ofpre-existing fissile material stockpiles.

This is a paradox. On the one hand, the US seems to take a leadership role in the global movement against nuclear proliferation and commits itself to achieve the goal of "a world without nuclear weapons" by proposing a verifiable FMCT. On the other hand, it has strong reservations aboutFMCT verification provisions that would include nuclear propulsion in strategic submarines and the involvement of the IAEA as the agency. This paradoxical approach of the US cannot be digested by the non-nuclear-weapon states and the G21 group of countries in the CD. The Trump administration's stance on FMCT negotiations remained the same as that of President Obama. Although the incumbent President Joe Biden has reiterated the need for the U.S. to lead, the wheels of the next significant nuclear non- proliferation treaty have not moved to the desired level. The US is unlikely to allow any intrusive verification that, they think, would compromise national security viz-a-viz its naval ship designs and configurations. Nevertheless, it considers thatbanning of production of fissile material through a consensus-driven FMCT would go a long way in realizing nuclear disarmament goals.

In conclusion, the research hasfound that FMCT negotiations are not progressing as desired, owing to conflicting interests and agendas among the CD-delegates. Even after more than 25 (twenty-five) years since President Clinton's proposed FMCT negotiations, member-states in the CD have been unable to resolve the major contentious issues. FMCT negotiations are in limbo, and the US poses one of the major hurdles to realizing an effective, verifiable, and non-discriminatory FMCT. The US approach to FMCT negotiations is amorphous as well as ambiguous.

India's stance on FMCT in the CD derives from its internal assessment of the long-term conventional and nuclear threats posed by two nuclear powers in the vicinity and the stance taken by powers such as the United States and other P-5 states. Concluding a successful FMCT is in the best interest of India, and it should continue to play an active role. India's future course of action shall depend on the decisions other key members in the CD make.

The book was written based on two hypotheses. The first hypothesis states, "The proposed FMCT serves as a stepping stone towards the goal of general and complete disarmament and, more particularly, nuclear disarmament." The second hypothesis states, "The proposed FMCT aims at an effective and non-discriminatory regime." The present research found these two hypotheses inadequate. They lack evidential findings to prove correct. Neither FMCT serves as a stepping stone towards the goal of nuclear disarmament, let alone the goal of general and complete disarmament, nor does FMCT aim at an effective and non-discriminatory regime.

Bibliography

Acton, James M. (2010), "Verifying Zero: Long Term Aims, Short-Term Steps", *UNODA Occasional Paper 18(3), Carnegie Endowment for International Peace,* January 1, [Online: web] Accessed 16 June 2014, URL: *http://carnegieendowment.org/2010/01/01/verifying-zero-long-term-aims-short-term-seps/xrw.*

Brenner, Michael J. (1981), *Nuclear Power and Non-Proliferation: The Remaking of US Policy,* New York: Cambridge University Press.

Berkhout, Frans *et al.* (1995), "A Cut-off in the Production of Fissile Material", *International Security, MIT Press,* Vol. 19 (3), 167-202.

Bunn, George (1998), "Making Progress on a Fissile Material Cut off Treaty after the South Asian Tests", *The Non-Proliferation Review,* 5 (3), 78-83.

Bunn, George (2003), "The Nuclear Nonproliferation Treaty: History and Current Problems", Arms Control Today, [Online: web] Accessed 10 September, 2013, URL: *http://www.armscontrol.org/act/2003_12/Bunn.*

Boese, Wade (2005), "Shunning the Table", *The American Prospect,* [Online: Web] Accessed 22 March 2014, URL: *http://prospect.org/article/shunning-table.*

Blix, Hans (2008), *Why Nuclear Disarmament Matters*, Cambridge: MIT Press.

Becker, Brian (2013), "US Nuclear Expansion Aims to Bully States: Analyst", Press TV, [Online: web] Accessed 1 April 2014, URL: *http://www.presstv.ir/detail/2013/12/23/341564/us-bullies-other-states-with-nexpansion/.*

Burgess, Marion Jr. (2010), *The Proposed Fissile Material Cut-off Treaty (FMCT) and its Potential Impact on US Navy Nuclear Propulsion*, Ph.D Thesis, California: Naval Post-Graduate School.

Chow, Brian G. *et al.* (1995), "The Proposed Fissile - Material Production Cutoff- Next Steps", *Rand Reports*, [Online: web] Accessed 16 August 2013, URL: *http://www.rand.org/pubs/monograph_reports/2007/MR586-1.pdf.*

*CRS Report for Congress (1997), Foreign Affairs and National Defense Division, Government of the United States of America, "Nuclear, Biological, Chemical, and Missile Proliferation Sanctions: Selected Current Law", *Prepared for the Subcommitee on International Security, Proliferation, and Federal Services of the US Senate Committee on Governmental Affairs*, November 25.

Cortell, Andrew P. and James W. Davis Jr. (2000), "Understanding the Domestic Impact of International Norms: A Research Agenda", *International Studies Review*, 2(1), 65-87.

*Conference on Disarmament (2002), "Working Paper on the Possible Scope and Requirements of the Fissile Material Treaty (FMT)", *From the Permanent Representative of South Africa to the CD*, CD/1671, 28 May, 2002.

*Conference on Disarmament (2003), "Working Paper on a Treaty to Ban the Production of Fissile Material for Nuclear Weapons and other Nuclear Explosive Devices", *Letter Dated 15 August 2003 from the Permanent Representatives of Japan to the Conference on Disarmament Addressed to the Secretary-General of the Conference (CD/1714)*, August 19, 2003.

*Conference on Disarmament (2009), "Draft for Discussion Prepared by the International Panel on Fissile Materials: A Treaty Banning the Production of Fissile Materials for Nuclear Weapons or Other Nuclear Explosive Devices, with article-by-article Explanations", *Letter Dated 16 September 2009 from the Permanent Representatives of Canada, Japan and the Netherlands to the Conference on Disarmament Addressed to the Secretary-General of the Conference,* December 15, 2009.

Caughley, Tim (2009), "Fissile Material Negotiations - Ways ahead", *United Nations Institute for Disarmament Research (UNIDIR),* [Online: web] Accessed on 5 July 2014, URL: *http://www.unidir.ch/files/conferences/pdfs/fissile-material-negotiations-ways-ahead-en-1-221.pdf.*

*Conference on Disarmament (2010), "Working Paper on Suggestions for the substance of the Fissile Material Cut-Off Treaty", *From the Permanent Representative of Australia to the CD,* CD/1895, 14 September, 2010.

*Conference on Disarmament (2011), "Working Paper on Fissile Material Cut-Off Treaty (FMCT)", *From the Permanent Representatives of Bulgaria, Germany, Mexico, Netherlands, Romania, Spain, Sweden and Turkey to the CD,* CD/1910, 9 June, 2011.

*Conference on Disarmament (2012), "the report of the meeting of scientific experts on technical issues related to a fissile material cut-off treaty (FMCT)", Tim Caughley Presentation II, titled, "Where do we stand on negotiating a fissile material treaty?" *Letter Dated 25 June from the Permanent Representatives of Germany and the Netherlands to the Conference on Disarmament addressed to the Secretary-General of the Conference (CD/1935),* June 26, 2012.

*Congressional Budget Office (CBO) (2013), Government of the United States of America, Congress of the United States, 'Projected Costs of US Nuclear Forces, 2014 to 2023', Pub. No. 4618, December: 1-12.

Council on Foreign Relations (2013), "The Global Nuclear

Nonproliferation Regime", *Issue Brief,* [Online: web] Accessed 25 March 2014, URL: *http://www.cfr.org/arms-control-disarmament-and-nonproliferation/global-nuclear-nonproliferation-regime/p18984#p4.*

Cirincione, Joseph (2013), "Obama's Nuclear Future: The Battle to Reduce the US Nuclear Stockpiles Begins", *Council on Foreign Relations,* [Online: web] Accessed 19 May 2014, URL: *http://www.foreignaffairs.com/articles/139037/joseph-cirincione/obamas-nuclear-future.*

Council on Foreign Affairs (2014), ""Nuclear Proliferation: Issue Brief" *Global Governance Monitor,* [Online: web] Accessed 25 March 2014, URL: *http://www.cfr.org/global-governance/global-governance-monitor/p18985#!/nuclear-proliferation.*

*Davis, Zachary and Warren Donnelly (1990), "Nuclear Proliferation Policy: A Compilation of Basic Documents on US Statutory and US Executive Branch Components of Non-Proliferation Policy", *CRS Report for Congress* [Online: web] Accessed 12 April 2014, URL: *http://www.dtic.mil/dtic/tr/fulltext/u2/a344609.pdf.*

Datan, Merav (2010), "Israel", in International Panel for Fissile Material (IPFM) Report *Reducing and Eliminating Nuclear Weapons: Country Perspectives on the Challenges to Nuclear Disarmament,* [Online: web] Accessed 18 May 2014, URL: *http://www.fissilematerials.org.*

Epstein, William (1990), "The Linkage Between a Nuclear Test-Ban and Nuclear Non-Proliferation", in M.P. Fry, N.P. Keatinge and J. Gotblat (eds.) Nuclear Non-proliferation and the Non-proliferation Treaty, Berlin: Springer-Verlag.

*Ford, Dr. Christopher A. (2007), Government of the United States of America, "The United States and Fissile Material Cutoff Treaty",*United States Special Representative for Nuclear Nonproliferation, delivered at the Conference on "Preparing for 2010: Getting the Process Right", Annecy, France, March 17, 2007, United States Department of State Archive 2001-2009, [Online: web] Accessed 29 July 2014, URL:http://2001-2009.state.gov/index.htm.*

Feiveson, Harold A. (2010), "Treatment of pre-existing fissile material stocks in an FM(C)T", in Theresa Hitchens and Jurg Lauber, *A Fissile Material Cutoff Treaty: Understanding the Critical Issues*, United Nations Institute for Disarmament Research (UNI Foust, Jeff (2010), "A change in tone in national space policy" *The Space Review*, [Online: web] Accessed 30 June 2014, URL: *http://www.thespacereview.com/article/1660/1.*

Graham, Thomas Jr. (2004), "Avoiding the Tipping Point", *Arms Control Association*, [Online: web] Accessed 1 June 2014, URL: *http://www.armscontrol.org/act/2004_11/*BookReview.

Glaser, Alexander (2012), "Facilitating Nuclear Disarmament: Verified Declarations of Fissile Material Stocks and Production", *The Non-Proliferation Review*, 19 (1), 125-135.

Hippel, Frank N. Von (1999), "The FMCT and Cuts in Fissile Material Stockpiles", *Disarmament Forum*, 13(2): 35-44.

Horovitz, Liviu and Robert Golan-Vilella (2010), "Comprehensive Nuclear-Test-Ban Treaty: How the Dominoes Might Fall after US Ratification", *The Nonproliferation Review*, 17 (2), 235-257.

Holloway, David (2010), "Nuclear Weapons and the Escalation of the Cold War, 1945-1962", in Melvyn P. Leffler and Odd Arne Westad (eds.) *The Cambridge History of the Cold War Vol. 1*, Cambridge: Cambridge University Press.

Hitchens, Theresa and Jurg Lauber (2010), "A Fissile Material Cutoff Treaty: Understanding the Critical Issues", *United Nations Institute for Disarmament Research (UNIDIR)*, United Nations Publications.

Holloway, David (2011), "The United States and the NPT "double bargain", in Olav Njolstad (ed.) *Nuclear Proliferation and International Order: Challenges to the Non-Proliferation Treaty*, New York: Routledge Publication.

*International Atomic Energy Agency (IAEA) (1953), "Atoms for Peace Speech", *Address by Mr. Dwight D. Eisenhower, President of the United States of America, to the 470th Plenary Meeting of the*

United Nations General Assembly, 8 December 1953, [Online: web] Accessed January 30, 2014, URL: http:/ www. iaea.org/About/ atomsforpeace_speech.html.

IPFM Draft (2009), "A Fissile Material (Cut-Off) Treaty (FMCT): A Treaty Banning the Production of Fissile Materials for Nuclear Weapons or Other Nuclear Explosive Devices", *International Panel for Fissile Materials*, [Online: web] Accessed 13 September 2013, URL: *http://fissilematerials.org/library/fmct-ipfm_feb2009draft.pdf.*

IAEA (2010), "IAEA safeguards and verification activities", in Theresa Hitchens and Jurg Lauber, *A Fissile Material Cutoff Treaty: Understanding the Critical Issues*, United Nations Institute for Disarmament Research (UNIDIR), Geneva: United Nations Publications.

Institute for Science and International Security (ISIS) (2013), "Ending the Production of Fissile Materials for Nuclear Weapons: Section VII", [Online: web] Accessed on 23 May, 2014, URL: *http://isis-online.org/section-7/.*

International Panel for Fissile Material (IPFM) (2020), "Countries: Russia", [Online: web] Accessed 27 May 2020, URL: *http:// fissilematerials.org/countries/russia.html.*

International Panel for Fissile Material (IPFM) (2020), "Countries: China", [Online: web] Accessed 27 May 2020, URL: *http:// fissilematerials.org/countries/china.html.*

Jonas, David S. (2006), "The New US Approach to the Fissile Material Cutoff Treaty: Will Deletion of a Verification Regime Provide the Way Out of the Wilderness?" *Florida Journal of International Law* XVIII.2: 597-678, [Online: web] Accessed 18 July 2013, *URL:http://works.bepress.com/david_jonas/3.*

Khan, Munir Ahmad (1990), "Towards a Universal Framework of Nuclear Restraint", in M.P. Fry, N.P. Keatinge and J. Gotblat (eds.) Nuclear Non-proliferation and the Non-proliferation Treaty, Berlin: Springer-Verlag.

Kristensen, Hans M. (2005), "New Doctrine Falls Short of Bush Pledge", *Arms Control Today*, [Online: web] Accessed 5 February 2014, URL: *http://www.armscontrol.org/act/2005_09/Kristensen.asp.*

Kimball, Daryl (2013), "Fissile Material Cut-off Treaty (FMCT) at a Glance", *Arms Control Today*, [Online: Web] Accessed 19 August 2013, URL: *http://www.armscontrol.org/factsheets/fmct.*

Medalia, Jonathan (1998), "Nuclear Weapons: Comprehensive Nuclear Test Ban Treaty and Nuclear Testing", *CRS Report for Congress, GlobalSecurity.org*, [Online: web] Accessed 29 January 2014, URL: *http://www.globalsecurity.org/wmd/library/report/crs/crs92099.htm.*

Ma, Chuyan and Frank N. von Hippel (2001), "Ending the Production of Highly Enriched Uranium for Naval Reactor," *The Non-Proliferation Review*, [Online: web] Accessed 15 August 2013, URL: *http://cns.miis.edu/npr/pdfs/81mahip.pdf.*

Meerburg, Arend and Frank N. von Hippel (2009), "Complete Cutoff: Designing a Comprehensive Fissile Material Treaty", *Arms Control Association*, [Online: web] Accessed 23 June 2014, URL: http://www.armscontrol.org/print/3546.

Mian, Zia *et al.* (2010), "India", in International Panel for Fissile Material (IPFM) Report *Reducing and Eliminating Nuclear Weapons: Country Perspectives on the Challenges to Nuclear Disarmament*, [Online: web] Accessed 18 May 2014, URL: *http://www.fissilematerials.org.*

Moller, Michael, JarmoSareva (2014), "Conference on Disarmament: Overview", *Nuclear Threat Initiative (NTI)*, [Online: web] Accessed 2 May, URL: *http://www.nti.org/treaties-and-regimes/conference-on-disarmament/.*

Nayan, Rajiv (2011), "India and the Fissile Material Cut-Off Treaty: Policy Options", *Strategic Analysis*, 35(1), 26-35.

Njolstad, Olav (2011), *Nuclear Proliferation and International Order: Challenges to the Non-Proliferation Treaty*, New York: Routledge.

*Nikitin, Mary Beth *et al.* (2012), "Proliferation Control Regimes: Background and Status", *Congressional Research Report (CRS), Library of the Congress,* RL31559.

Nuclear Threat Initiative (NTI) (2013), "Proposed Fissile Material (Cut-off) Treaty (FMCT)", [Online: web] Accessed 3 June 2013, URL: *http://www.nti.org/treaties-and-regimes/proposed-fissile-material-cut-off-reaty/*

Nuclear Threat Initiative (NTI) (2018), "Proposed Fissile Material (Cut-off) Treaty (FMCT)", [Online: web] Accessed 9 June 2019, URL: *https://www.nti.org/learn/treaties-and-regimes/proposed-fissile-material-cut-off-treaty/*

*Office of the Press Secretary (2009), "Remarks by President Barack Obama at the Hradcany Square, Prague, Czech Republic", April 5, 2009, *The White House,* [Online: web] Accessed 16 March 2014, URL: *http://www.whitehouse.gov/the_press_office/Remarks-By-President-Barack-Obama-In-Prague-As-Delivered.*

*Office of the Historian (2013 a), "Milestones 1945-52: The Acheson-Lilienthal & Baruch Plans, 1946", *US Department of State,* [Online: web] Accessed 10 September, 2013, URL: *http://history.state.gov/milestones/1945-1952/BaruchPlans.*

*Office of the Historian (2013 b), "Milestones 1961-68: The Nuclear Non-Proliferation Treaty (NPT), 1968", *US Department of State,* [Online: web] Accessed 10 September, 2013, URL: *http://history.state.gov/milestones/1961-1968/npt.*

*Office of the Historian (2014 a), Government of the United States of America, US Department of State, *'Milestones: 1945-1952, The Acheson-Lilienthal & Baruch Plans, 1946',* [Online: web] Accessed 19 January 2014, URL: *https://history.state.gov/milestones/1945-1952/baruch-plans.*

*Office of the Historian (2014 b), Government of the United States of America, US Department of State, *'Milestones: 1961-68, The Limited Test Ban Treaty, 1963',* [Online: web] Accessed

19 January 2014, URL: *http://history.state.gov/milestones/1961-1968/limited-ban.*

*Office of the Historian (2014 c), Government of the United States of America, US Department of State, *'Milestones: 1961-68, The Nuclear Non-Proliferation Treaty, 1968'*, [Online: web] Accessed 2 February 2014, URL: *http://history.state.gov/milestones/1961-1968/limited-ban.*

Persbo, Andreas (2010), "A verified ban on fissile material production", in Hitchens, Theresa and Jurg Lauber (eds.), *A Fissile Material Cutoff Treaty: Understanding the Critical Issues,* Geneva: United Nations Institute for Disarmament Research (UNIDIR), United Nations Publications.

Pellaud, Bruno (2010), "Focussing on FMCT Verification", in Theresa Hitchens and Jurg Lauber, *A Fissile Material Cutoff Treaty: Understanding the Critical Issues,* United Nations Institute for Disarmament Research (UNIDIR), Geneva: United Nations Publications.

Roberts, Guy (2001), "This Arms Control Dog Won't Hunt: the Proposed Fissile Material Cut-Off Treaty at the Conference on Disarmament", *USAF Institute for National Security Studies,* INSS Occasional Paper 36, 1-63.

Reif, Kingston and Madeleine Foley (2009), "Fact Sheet on the Fissile Material Cutoff Treaty (FMCT)", *The Center for Arms Control and Non-Proliferation,* [Online: web] Accessed 1 August 2013, URL: *http://armscontrolcenter.org/issues/nuclearweapons/articles/071509_factsheet_fmct/.*

Reif, Kingston (2009), "Factsheet on the Fissile Material Cutoff Treaty (FMCT), *The Center for Arms Control and Non-Proliferation,* [Online: web] Accessed 15 May 2014, URL: *http://armscontrolcenter.org/issues/iran/articles/071509_factsheet_fmct/.*

Ritchie, Nick (2009), *US Nuclear Weapons Policy after the Cold War: Russians, 'rogues' and domestic division,* New York: Routledge.

Reif, Kingston and Madeleine Foley (2013), "Fact Sheet on the Fissile Material Cut-off Treaty (FMCT)", *The Center for Arms*

Control and Non-Proliferation, [Online: web] Accessed 24 October 2013, URL: *http://armscontrolcenter.org/publications/factsheets/071509_factsheet_fmct/*.

Reaching Critical Will (RCW) (2014 a), "Conference on Disarmament", [Online: web] Accessed 6 June 2014, URL: *http://www.reachingcriticalwill.org/disarmament-fora/cd*.

Reaching Critical Will (RCW) (2014 b), "Outer Space: Militarization, weaponization, and the prevention of an arms race", [Online: web] Accessed 26 June 2014, URL: *http://reachingcriticalwill.org/resources/fact-sheets/critical-issues/5448-outer-space#ppwt*.

Simpson, John (1985), "The Non- Proliferation Treaty at its Half-life", in Ian Bellany, Coit D. Blacker and Joseph Gallacher (eds.) *The Nuclear Non-Proliferation Treaty*, London: Frank Cass and Co Ltd.

Sethi, Manpreet (1998), "The Fissile Material Cut off Debate", *Strategic Analysis*, 22 (9), 1381-1391.

Schaper, Annette and Harald Muller (2004), "US Nuclear Policy after the Cold War", *Peace Research Institute Frankfurt (PRIF)*, PRIF Reports No. 69.

*Squassoni, Sharon, *et al.* (2006), "Banning Fissile Material Production for Nuclear Weapons: Prospects for a Treaty (FMCT)", *CRS Report for Congress*, [Online: web] Accessed 30 November, 2013, URL: *http://www.fas.org/sgp/crs/nuke/RS22474.pdf*.

Squassoni, Sharon (2008), "Looking Back: The 1978 Nuclear Nonproliferation Act", Arms Control Today, [Online: web] Accessed 5 January, 2013, URL: *https://www.armscontrol.org/act/2008_12/lookingback_NPT*.

Schaper, Annette (2010), "A Treaty of Fissile Materials: Just Cut-off of More?", in Hitchens, Theresa and Jurg Lauber (eds.), *A Fissile Material Cutoff Treaty: Understanding the Critical Issues*, United Nations Institute for Disarmament Research (UNIDIR), Geneva: United Nations Publications.

Singal, Amel (2011), Bringing North Korea Back into the NPT Regime", in Olav Njolstad (ed.) Nuclear Proliferation and International Order: Challenges to the Non-Proliferation Treaty, New York: Routledge.

Stockholm International Peace Research Institute (SIPRI) (2013), *SIPRI Yearbook 2013: Armaments, Disarmament and International Security*, Solna: Oxford University Press.

*"Text of the Nuclear Non-Proliferation Treaty" (1968), *Federation of American Scientists*, [Online: web], Accessed 27 July, 2013, URL: *http://www.fas.org/nuke/control/npt/text/*.

Tellis, Ashley J. (2001), *India's Emerging Nuclear Posture: Between Recessed Deterrent and Ready Arsenal*, Santa Monica: Rand Corporation.

*The White House (2006), Government of the United States of America, "US National Space Policy", *Office of the Press Secretary*, [Online: web] Accessed 3 July 2014, URL: *http://www.whitehouse.gov/sites/default/files/microsites/ostp/national-space-policy-2006.pdf*.

*The White House (2009), Government of the United States, "Remarks by the President Barack Obama In Prague As Delivered", *Office of the Press Secretary*, 5 April [Online: web] Accessed 23 March 2014, URL: *http://www.whitehouse.gov/the_press_office/Remarks-By-President-Barack-Obama-In-Prague-As-Delivered/*.

*The White House (2010), Government of the United States of America, "Fact Sheet: The National Space Policy", *Office of the Press Secretary*, [Online: web] Accessed 3 July 2014, URL: *http://www.whitehouse.gov/the-press-office/fact-sheet-national-space-policy*.

*US Department of State (1993), "Address by the President Bill Clinton to the UN General Assembly (New York)", September 27 1993, *Bureau of International Organization Affairs*, [Online: web] Accessed 3 April 2013, URL: *http://www.state.gov/p/io/potusunga/207375.htm*.

*US Department of State (2013 a), "Remarks by the Secretary of State Hillary Rodham Clinton at the Review Conference of the Nuclear Security Summit (New York)", May 3, 2010, *Bureau of International Security and Nonproliferation (ISN)*, [Online: web] Accessed 4 April 2013, URL: *http://www.state.gov/t/isn/index.htm.*

*US Department of State (2013 b), *Bureau of International Security and Non-Proliferation (ISN)*, Government of the United States of America, Washington D.C.

*US Department of State (2013 c), "Overview: Nuclear Non-proliferation Treaty", *Bureau of International Security and Nonproliferation (ISN)*, [Online: web] Accessed February 20 2014, URL: *http://www.state.gov/t/isn/npt/.*

*US Department of State (2014), "Joint Statement on the Contributions of the Global Initiative to Combat Nuclear Terrorism (GICNT) to Enhancing Nuclear Security", *Office of the Spokesperson*, URL: *http://www.state.gov)/r/pa/prs/ps/2014/03/223761.htm.*

*US Mission to the United Nations in Geneva (2006), "United States of America White Paper on Fissile Material Cutoff Treaty", *Press Release*, [Online: web] Accessed 30 March 2014, URL: *http://fissilematerials.org/library/usm06.pdf.*

*US Mission to the United Nations in Geneva (2010), "Ambassador Laura Kennedy: US is Eager for the CD to Again Make an Active Contribution to Disarmament", *Statement to the Conference on Disarmament by Ambassador Laura Kennedy and US Special Representative for Biological and Toxin Weapons Convention Issues*, 23 March, [Online: web] Accessed 22 June 2014, URL: *https://geneva.usmission.gov/2010/03/23/cd-statement/.*

*US Mission to the United Nations in Geneva (2011), "Ambassador Laura Kennedy's CD Statement on Space Policy"*Statement by the Delegation of the United States to theConference on DisarmamentDelivered byAmbassador Laura Kennedy,Permanent Representative to the Conference on*

DisarmamentAndUS Special Representative for Biological and Toxin Weapons Convention Issues, 8 February, [Online: web] Accessed 3 July 2014, URL: *https://geneva.usmission.gov/2011/02/08/ambassador-kennedy-space-policy/.*

*US Mission to the United Nations in Geneva (2011 a), "Transcript of Press Briefing with Assistant Secretary Rose Gottemoeller", *Statement by **Assistant Secretary Rose Gottemoeller**US Bureau of Arms Control, Verification and Compliance,* 27 January, [Online: web] Accessed 22 June 2014, URL: *https://geneva.usmission.gov/2011/01/28/transcript-rose-gottemoeller/.*

*US Mission to the United Nations in Geneva (2011 b), "US Statement at the CD on a Fissile Material Cutoff Treaty (FMCT)", *Statement by the Delegation of the United States to the Conference on DisarmamentDelivered byJeffrey Eberhardt Director, Office of Nuclear AffairsThe Department of State,* 3 February, [Online: web] Accessed 22 June 2014, URL: *https://geneva.usmission.gov/2011/02/09/fmctreaty/.*

*US Mission to the United Nations in Geneva (2011 c), "Ambassador Kennedy on the Fissile Material Cut-off Treaty (FMCT)", ***Statement by Ambassador Laura Kennedy,Permanent Representative to the Conference on DisarmamentAndUS Special Representative for Biological and Toxin Weapons Convention Issues,*** March 3, [Online: web] Accessed 3 July 2014, URL: *https://geneva.usmission.gov/2011/03/03/ambassador-kennedy-on-the-fissile-material-cut-off-treaty-fmct/.*

* US Mission to the United Nations in Geneva (2012), "Assistant Secretary of State Gottemoeller Delivers US Opening Statement at Conference on Disarmament", *Assistant Secretary of State Rose Gottemoelle rOpening Statement at the Conference on DisarmamentGeneva, SwitzerlandAs Delivered,24 January,*[Online: web] Accessed 3 July 2014, URL: *https://geneva.usmission.gov/2012/01/24/gottemoeller-conference-on-disarmament/.*

*US Mission to the United Nations in Geneva (2013 a), "Ambassador Kennedy's Statement to the Conference on

Disarmament", *Statement by United States Ambassador Laura Kennedy To the Conference on Disarmament*, 5 March, [Online: web] Accessed 22 June 2014, URL: *https://geneva.usmission.gov/2013/03/05/ambassadorkennedys-statement-to-the-conference-on-disarmament/*.

*US Mission to the United Nations in Geneva (2013 b), "Ambassador Kennedy: the CD should Initiate FMCT Negotiations as soon as Possible", *Statement to the Conference on Disarmament Delivered by Ambassador Laura Kennedy,*

US Permanent Representative to the Conference on Disarmament *and US Special Representative for Biological and Toxin Weapons Convention Issues,* March 12, [Online: web] Accessed 22 April 2014, URL: *https://geneva.usmission.gov/2013/03/12/ambassador-kennedy-on/*.

*US Mission to the United Nations in Geneva (2013 c), "Ambassador Kennedy's Final Statement in the CD", *Statement by Ambassador Laura Kennedy to the Conference on Disarmament and US Special Representative for Biological and Toxin Weapons Convention Issues*, 24 May, [Online: web] Accessed 22 June 2014, URL: *https://geneva.usmission.gov/2013/05/26/ambassadors-final-statement-in-the-cd/*.

*US Mission to the United Nations in Geneva (2014), "Acting Under Secretary Gottemoeller: Negotiation for an FMCT an Essential Prerequisite for Global Nuclear Disarmament", *Statement by Rose E. GottemoellerActing Under Secretary of State for Arms Control and International SecurityConference on Disarmament,*4 February, [Online: web] Accessed 22 June 2014, URL: *https://geneva.usmission.gov/2014/02/04/acting-under-secretary-gottemoeller-negotiation-of-an-fmct-an-essential-prerequisite-for-global-nuclear-disarmament/*.

*US Mission to the United Nations in Geneva (2019), "Ambassador Robert Woods'CD Remark on Fissile Material Cut-Off Treaty", *Statement by United States on the Conference on Disarmament*, 8 August, [Online: web] Accessed 8 March 2020,

URL: *https://geneva.usmission.gov/2019/08/09/ambassador-robert-woods-cd-remarks-on-fissile-material-cut-off-treaty.*

United States Institute of Peace (2009), *America's Strategic Posture: The Final Report of the Congressional Committee on the Strategic Posture of the United States,* May 2009, United States Institute of Peace Press: Washington D.C.

*Under Secretary for Arms Control and International Security (2006), Government of the United States of America, US Department of State, "Texts of the Draft Mandate for Negotiations and the Draft Treaty – Conference on Disarmament", *Bureau of International Security and Nonproliferation (ISN),* [Online: web] Accessed 2 May 2014, URL: *http://2001-2009.state.gov/t/isn/rls/other/66902.htm.*

*US Nuclear Regulatory Commission (USNRC) (2013 a), Government of the United States, Department of Energy, 'Nuclear Non-Proliferation Act', *Nuclear Regulatory Legislation, 112th Congress; 2nd Session,* 3 (10), March 10: 1073.

*United States Nuclear Regulatory Commission (US NRC) (2013 b), Government of the United States of America, "Special Nuclear Material", *Nuclear Materials,* [Online: web] Accessed 30 March 2014, URL: *http://www.nrc.gov/materials/sp-nucmaterials.html.*

*Under Secretary for Arms Control and International Security (2014), Government of the United States of America, US Department of State, 'Nuclear Proliferation Treaty', *Bureau of International Security and Nonproliferation (ISN),* [Online: web] Accessed 3 May 2014, URL: *http://www.state.gov/t/isn/npt.*

*United Nations Office for Disarmament Affairs (UNODA) (2014), "Treaty on the Nonproliferation of Nuclear Weapons", [Online: web] Accessed February 20 2014, URL: *http://www.un.org/disarmament/WMD/Nuclear/NPT.shtml.*

*Woolf, Amy F. (2003), "Nuclear Weapons and US National Security: A Need for New Weapons Programs?" *CSR Report for Congress,* RS21619.

*Woolf, Amy F. (2008), "Nuclear Weapons in the US National Security Policy: Past, Present and Prospects", *Congressional Research Report (CRS), Library of the Congress,* RL34226.

Warren, Aiden (2011), "The Promises of Prague versus Nuclear Realities: From Bush to Obama", *Contemporary Security Policy,* 32 (2), 432-457.

*Woolf, Amy F. *et al.* (2013), "Arms Control and Nonproliferation: A Catalog of Treaties and Agreements", *Congressional Research Report (CRS), Library of the Congress,* RL33865.

Index